In late 2012 an acquaintance and I were passing time at work and the topic of thrift stores came up. She claimed that while she loved thrift shopping she hated shopping at the Deseret Industries chain of thrift stores because they're owned by Mormons.

Petty bigotry aside, Utah has a vibrant thrift community. Salt Lake City and the surrounding areas like Provo and Ogden are composed of a solid middle-class population with lots of students and families. There's thousands of people getting rid of stuff and even more looking to snatch it up. While savvy Utah thrift shoppers may be aware of a few Savers or Goodwill stores in Utah, the Utah thrift store scene is dominated by Deseret Industries.

Deseret Industries is, in fact, run by the Church of Jesus Christ of Latter Day Saints (LDS)- perhaps better known as the Mormons. They try, from all appearances, to hire folks that need a hand at times, and if we can judge by the employees outside smoking cigarettes on break, Deseret Industries employee qualifications do not include active membership in the Mormon church.

I was bugged by my acquaintances' casual discrimination. In Utah, it's acceptable to broadcast hate in a certain direction. It's okay to say, "I don't like shopping there because it's owned by Mormons." If one were to replace "Mormons" with "blacks" or "Jews" or "Asians" they'd be called out immediately as racist. For some reason though in Utah it's okay to be hostile to a religious group if that group is the Mormons.

As I pondered our exchange later that same day, I realized that since high school I'd been shopping at Deseret Industries and other thrift stores. Call me cheap. I like second hand stuff. I thought I'd been to most of the Deseret Industries stores and thought I could remember most of them. Salt Lake City, Provo, St. George, etc. I decided to visit them all again - to reassess the state of second hand stuff in Utah.

I was shocked when I found Deseret Industries stores spread across the entire Western United States; Washington, Oregon, Idaho, California, Nevada, Arizona, and, of course, Utah. There were (when I started trying to visit them all) 43 stores in 7 different western states.

I spent over a year driving to them all.

I took photos at each one.

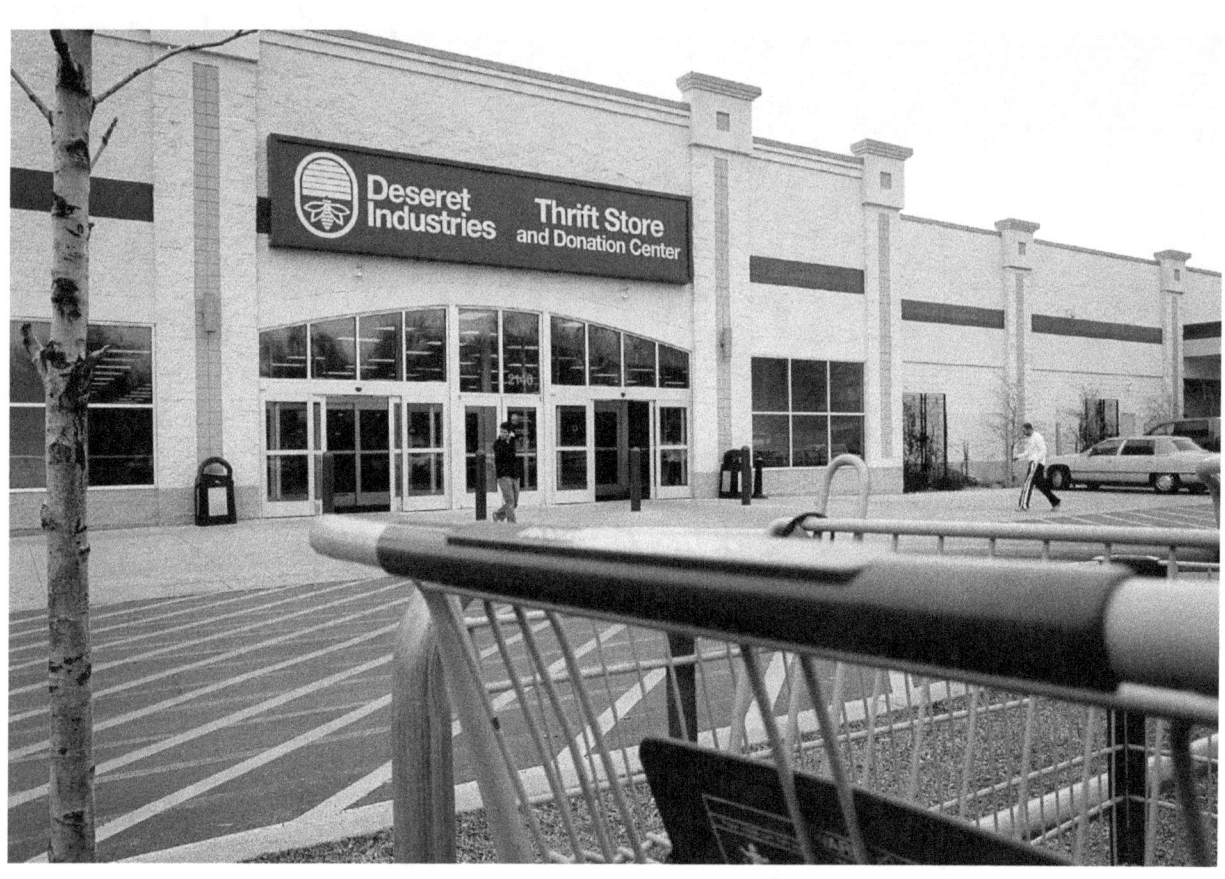

Sugarhouse, Utah

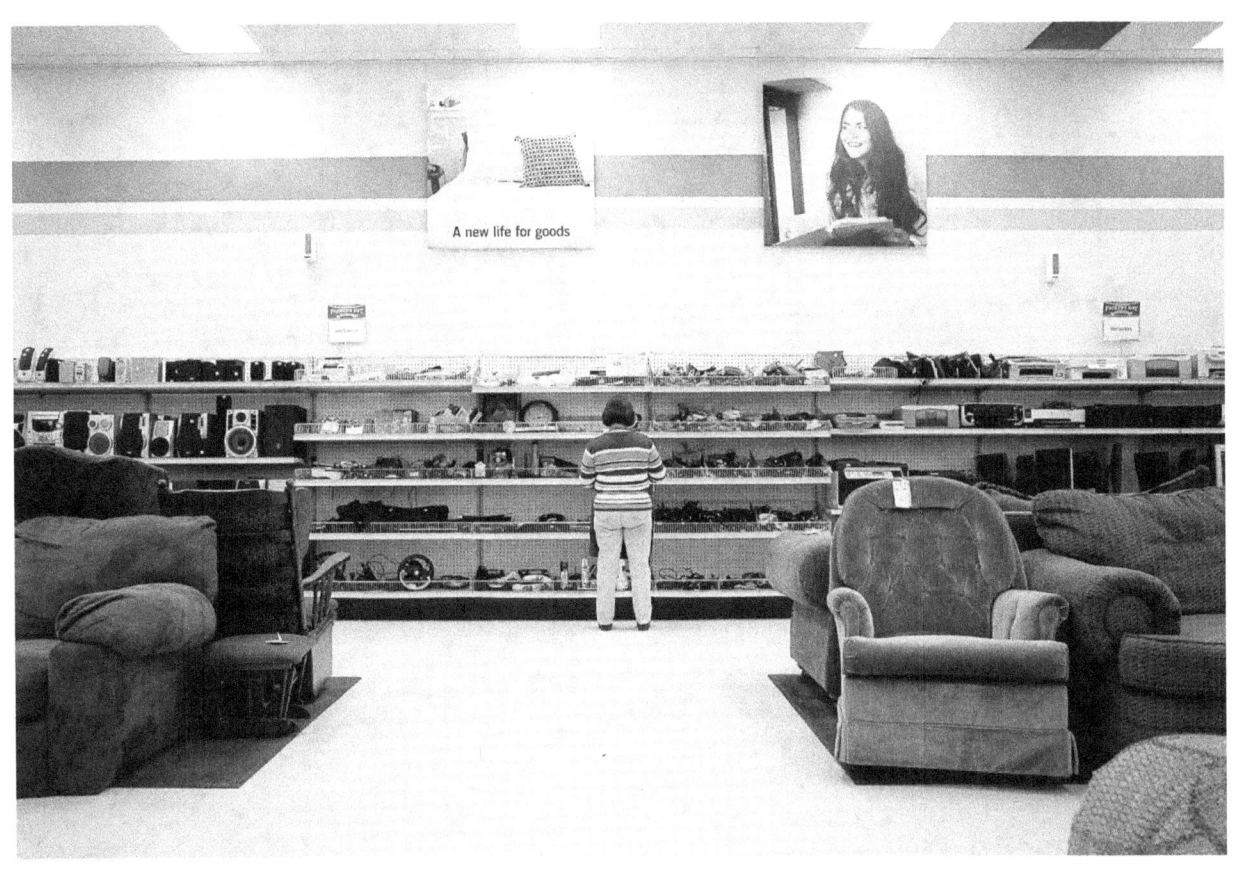

A new life for goods

Harrisville, Utah

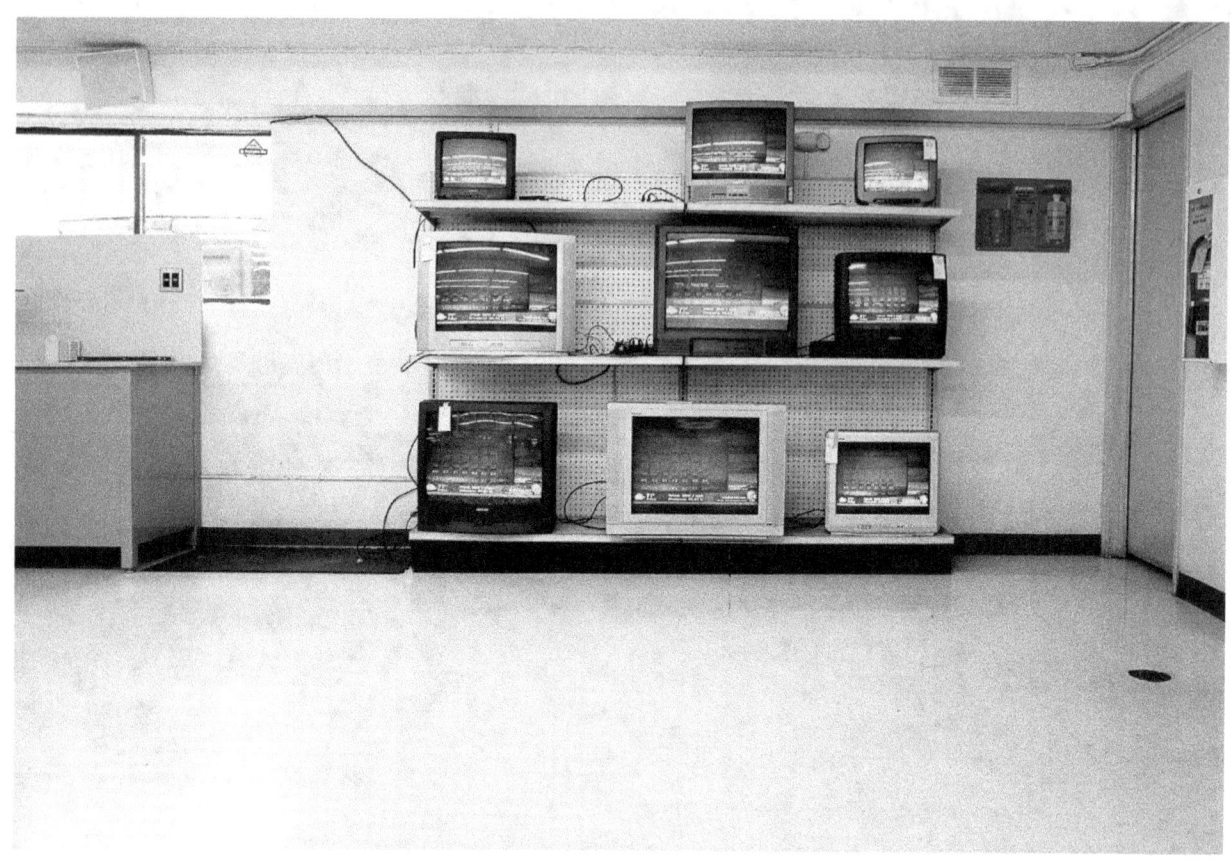

Cedar City, Utah

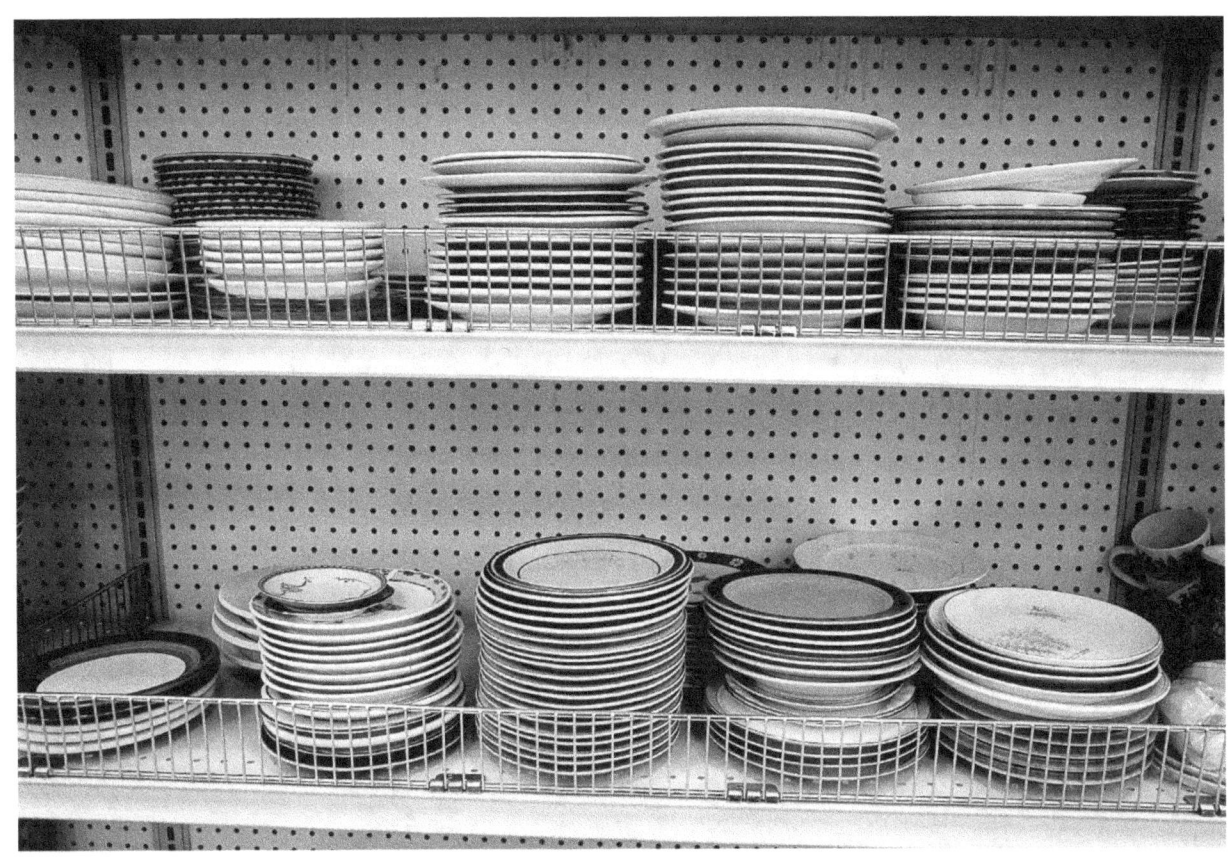

Twin Falls, Idaho

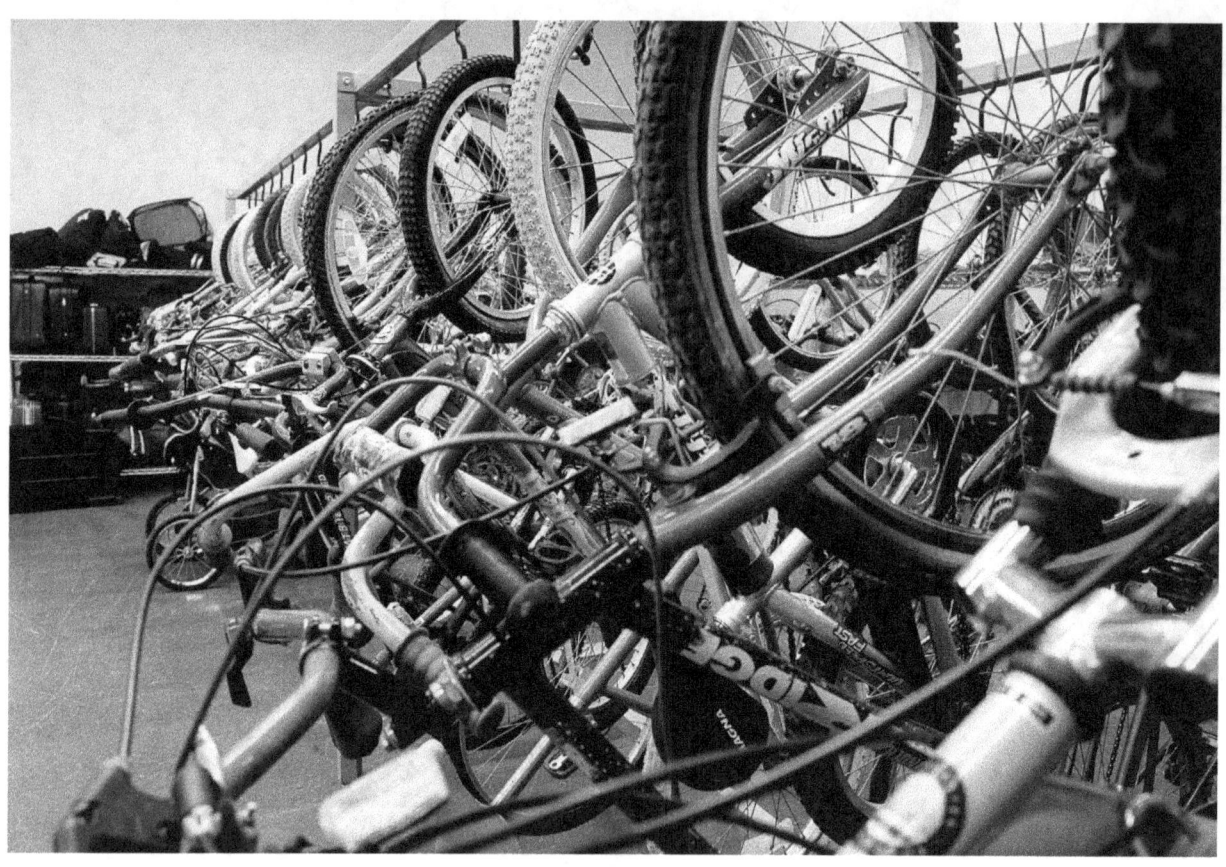

Logan, Utah

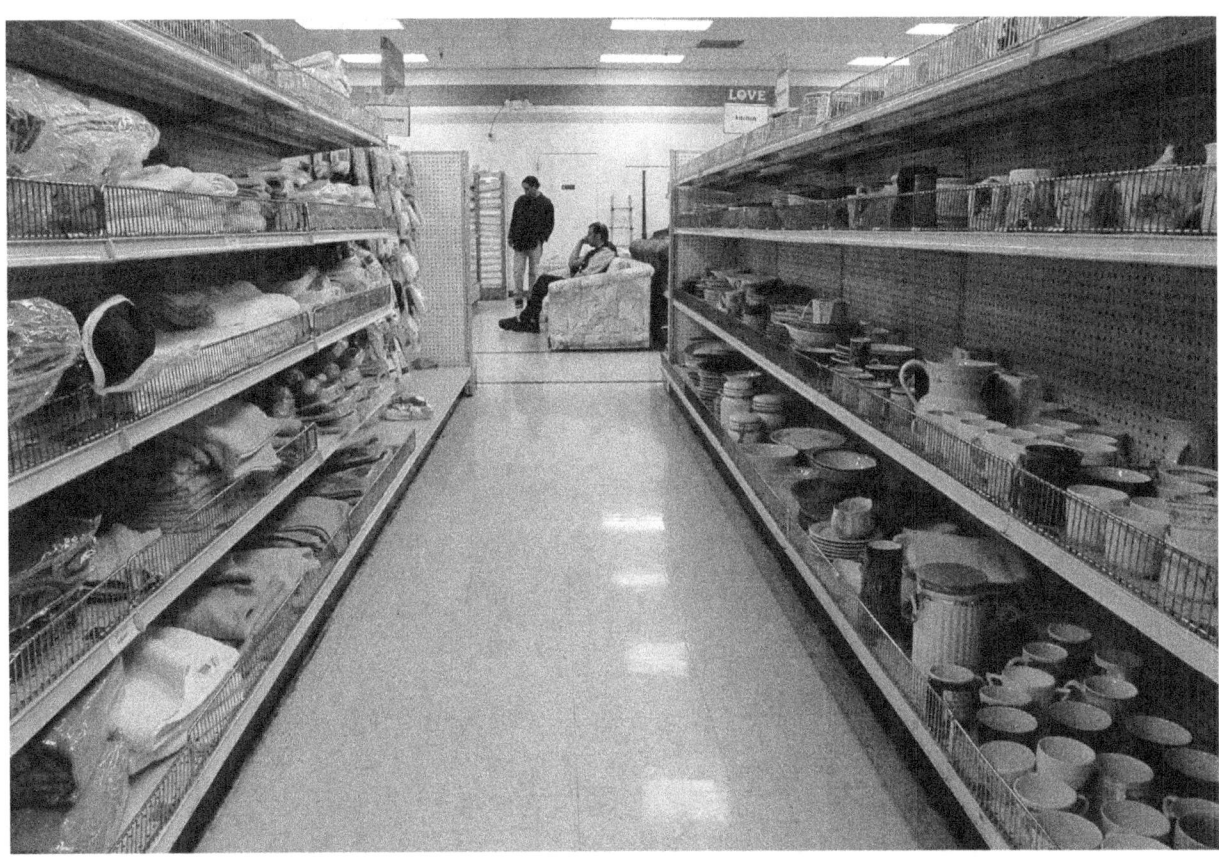

Mesa, Arizona

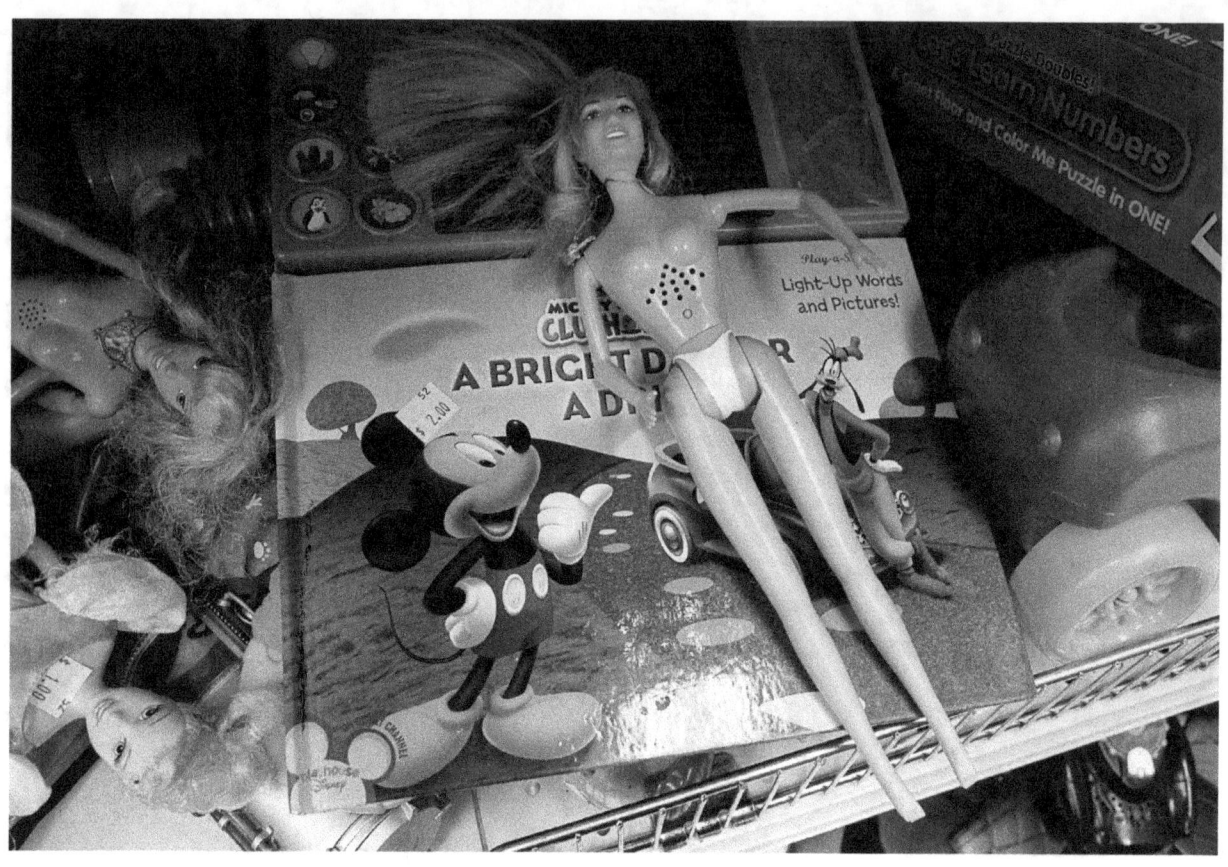

Blackfoot, Idaho

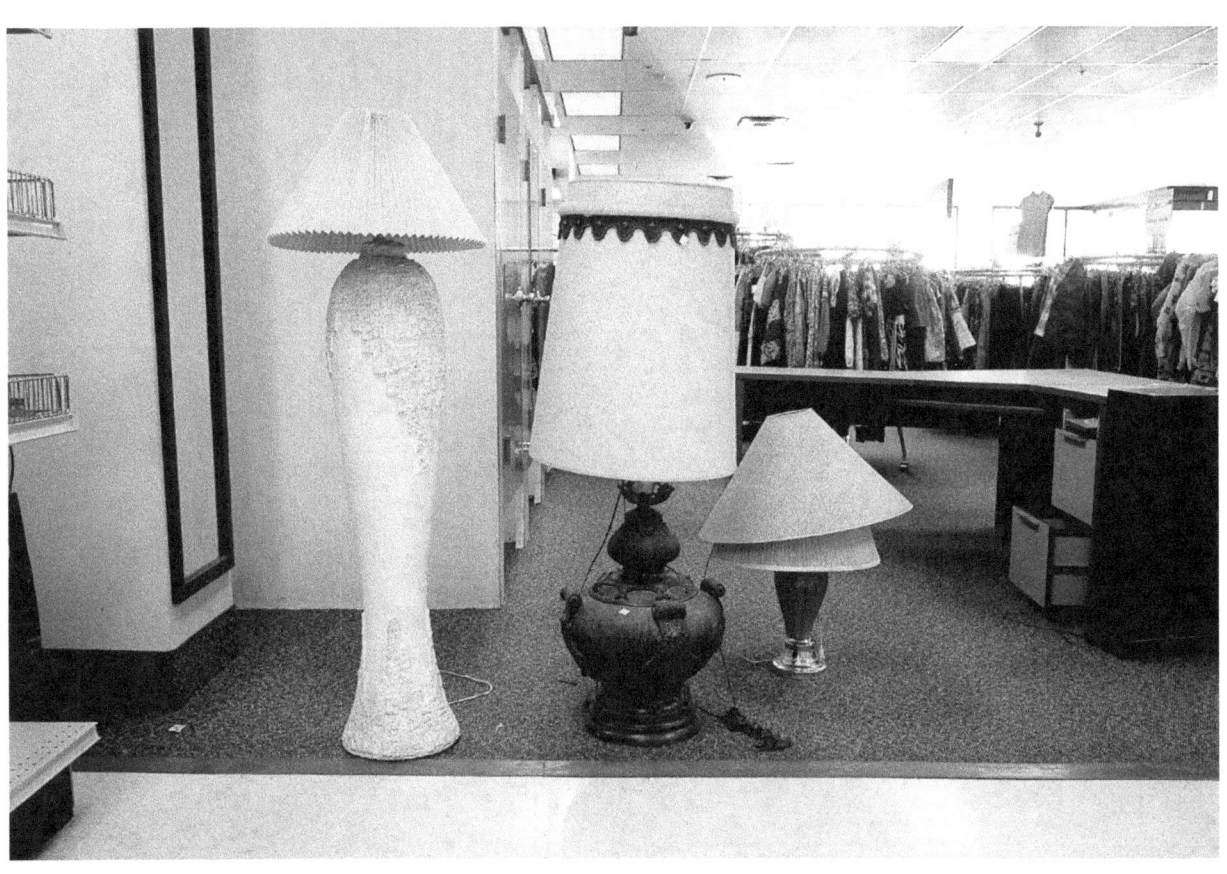

Price, Utah

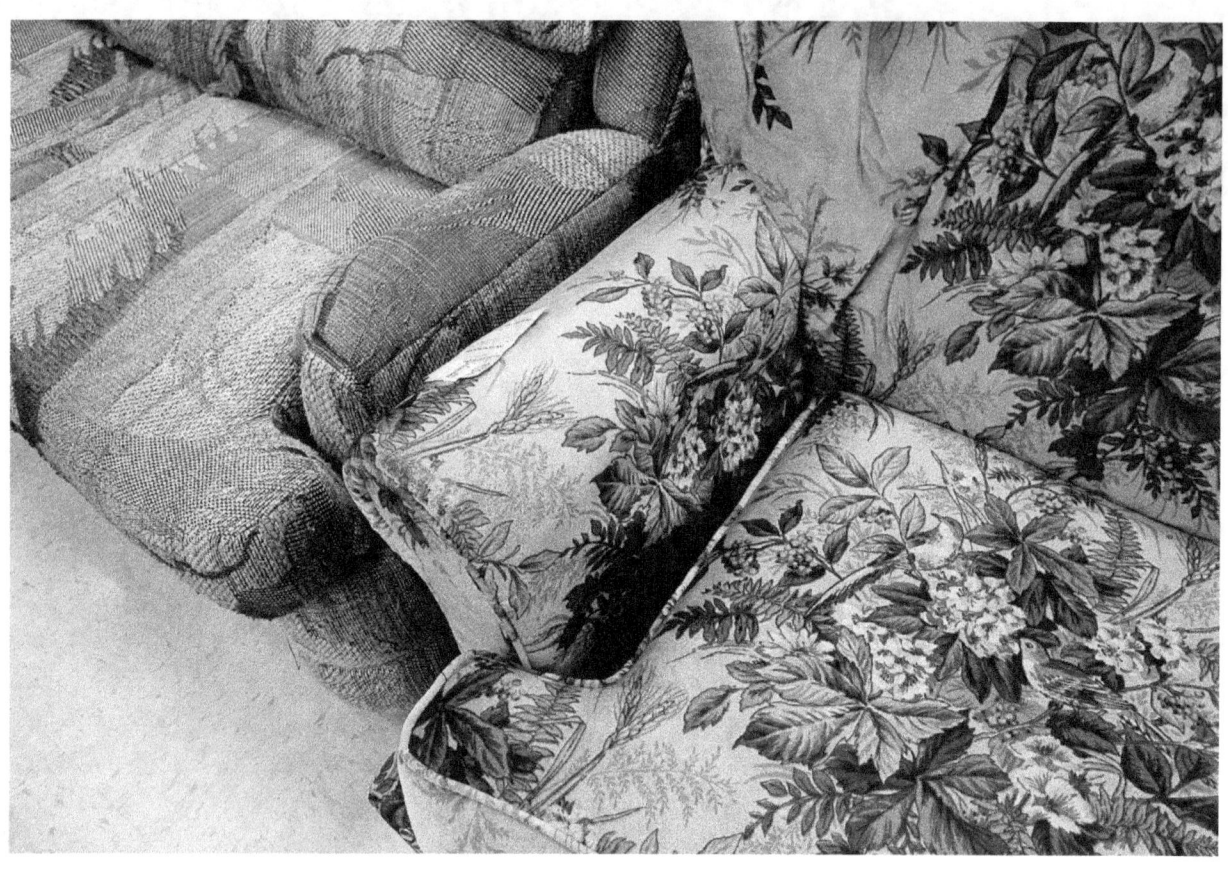

Logan, Utah

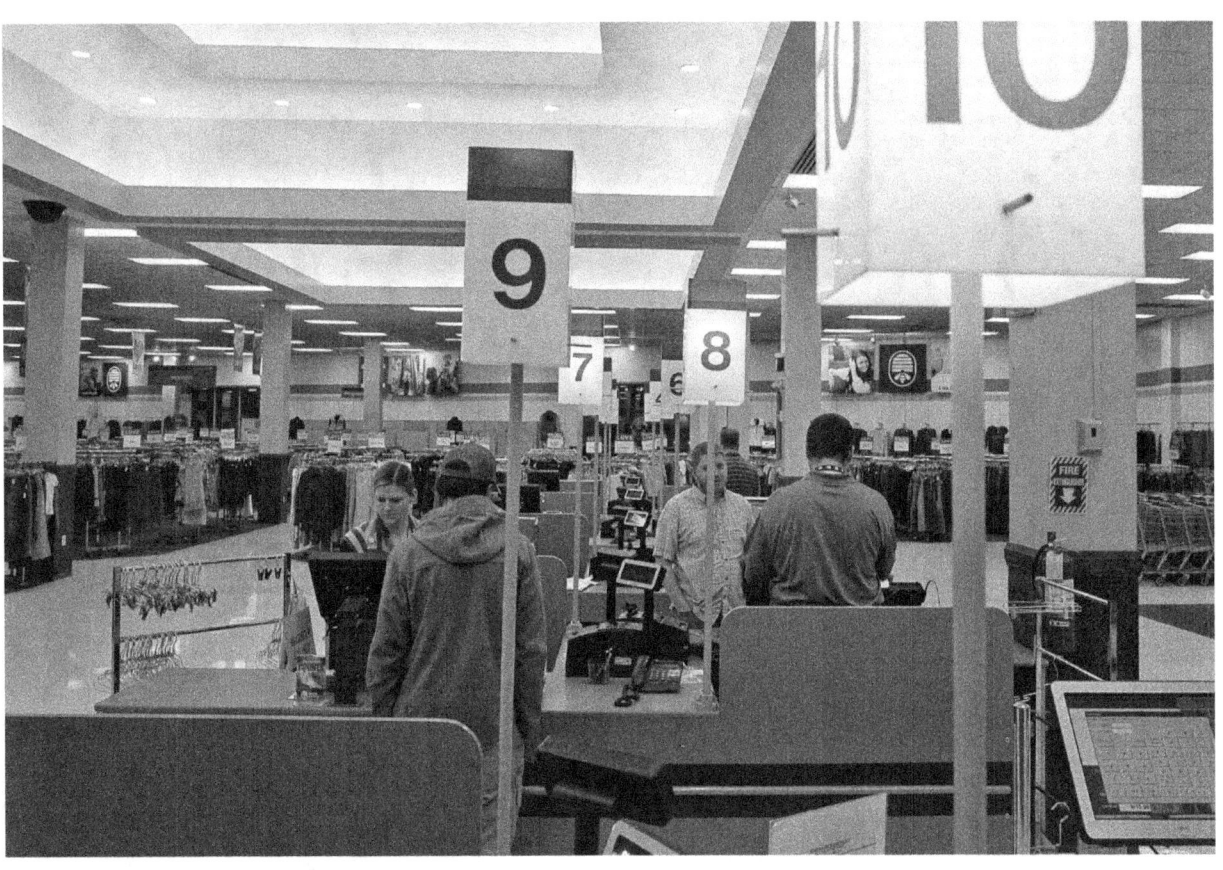

Provo, Utah

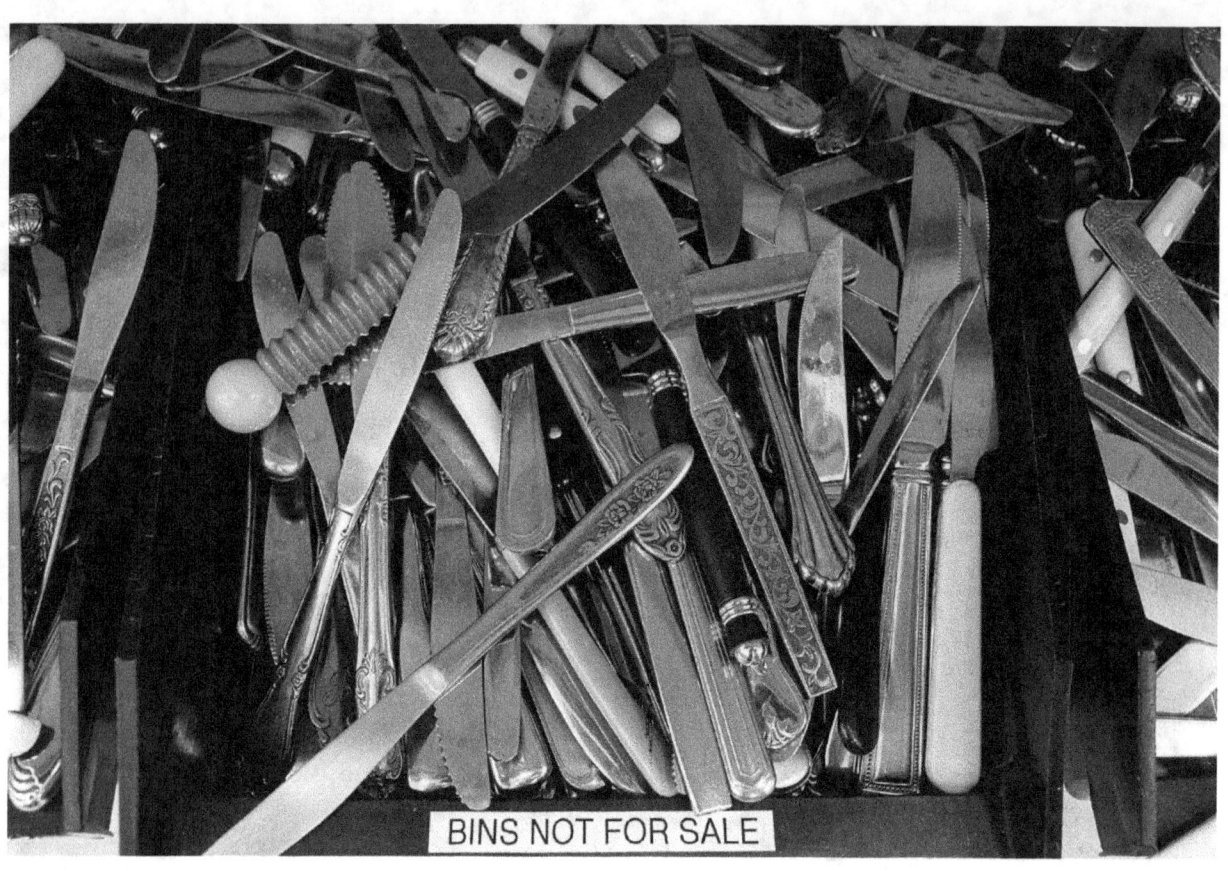

American Fork, Utah

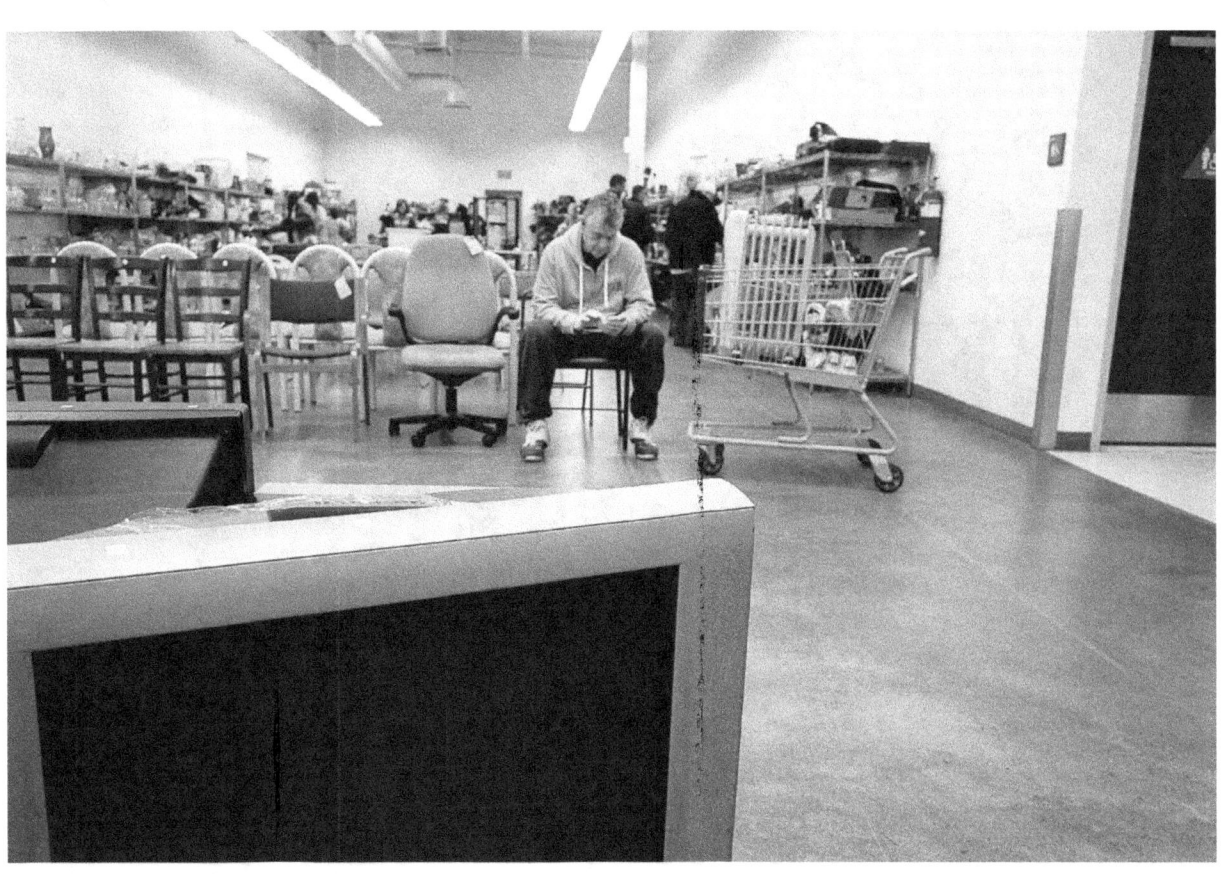

Sugarhouse, Utah

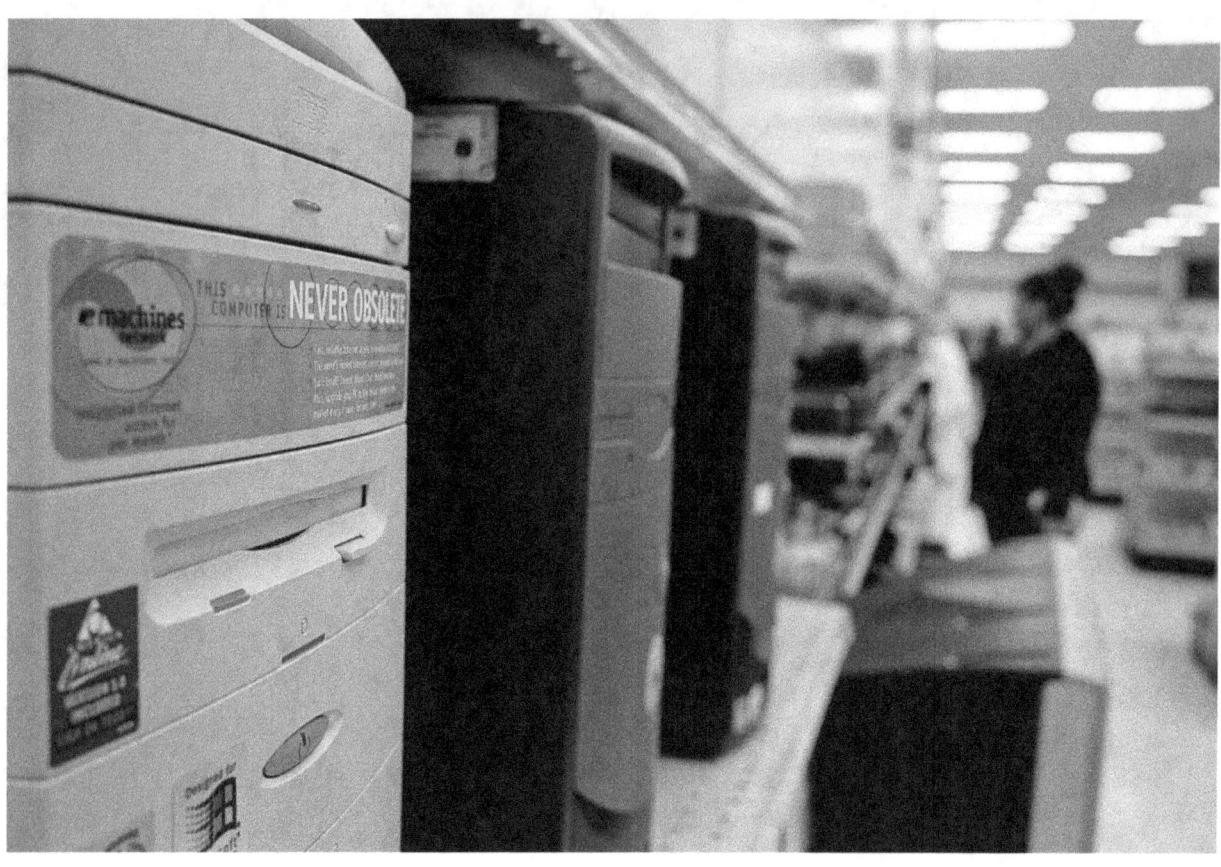

Provo, Utah

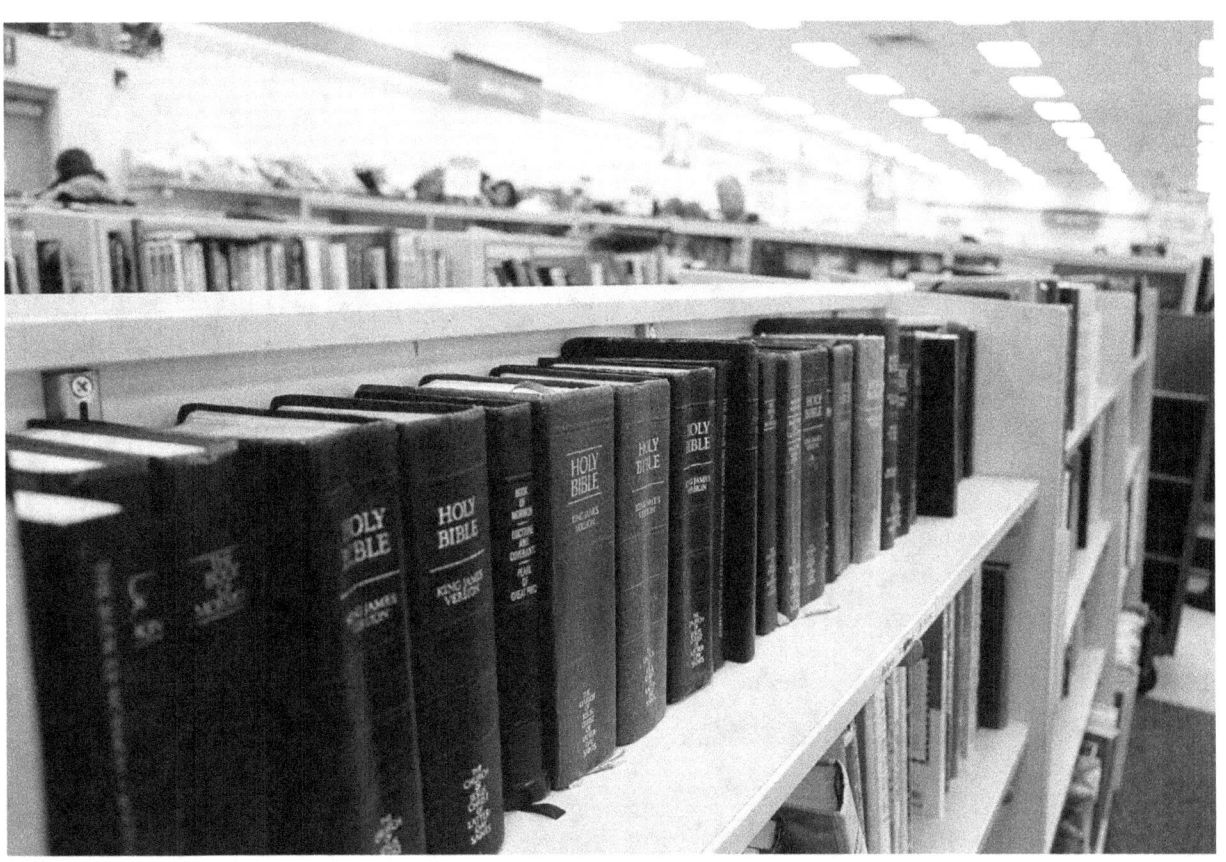

American Fork, Utah

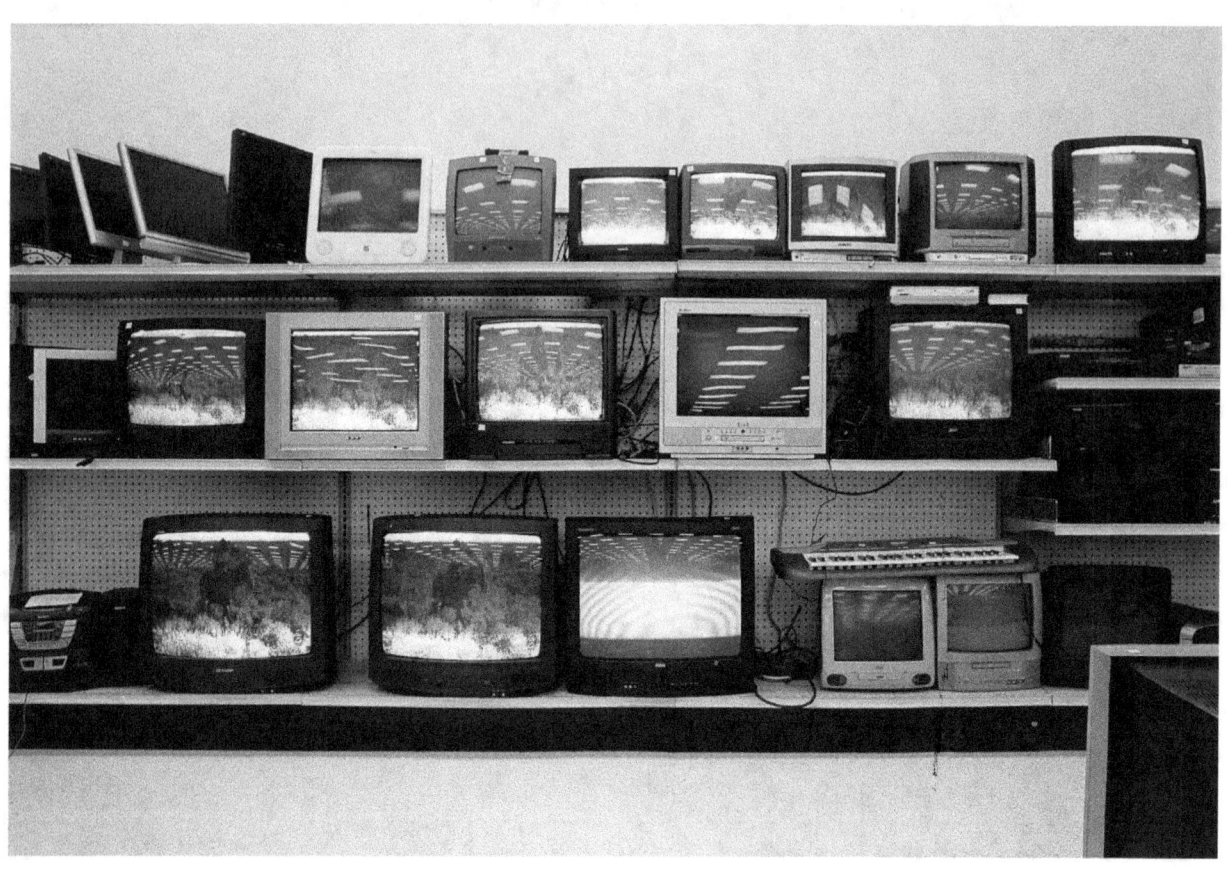

Sacramento, California

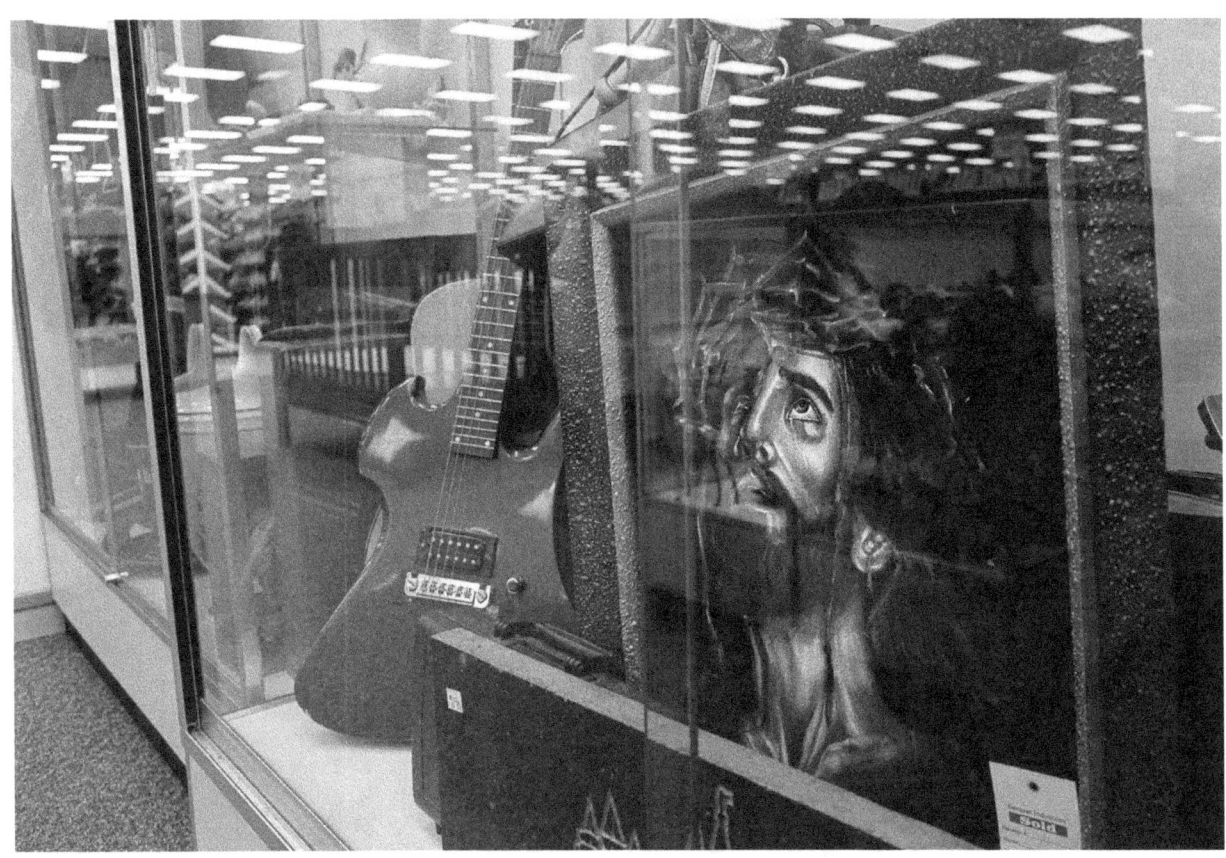

American Fork, Utah

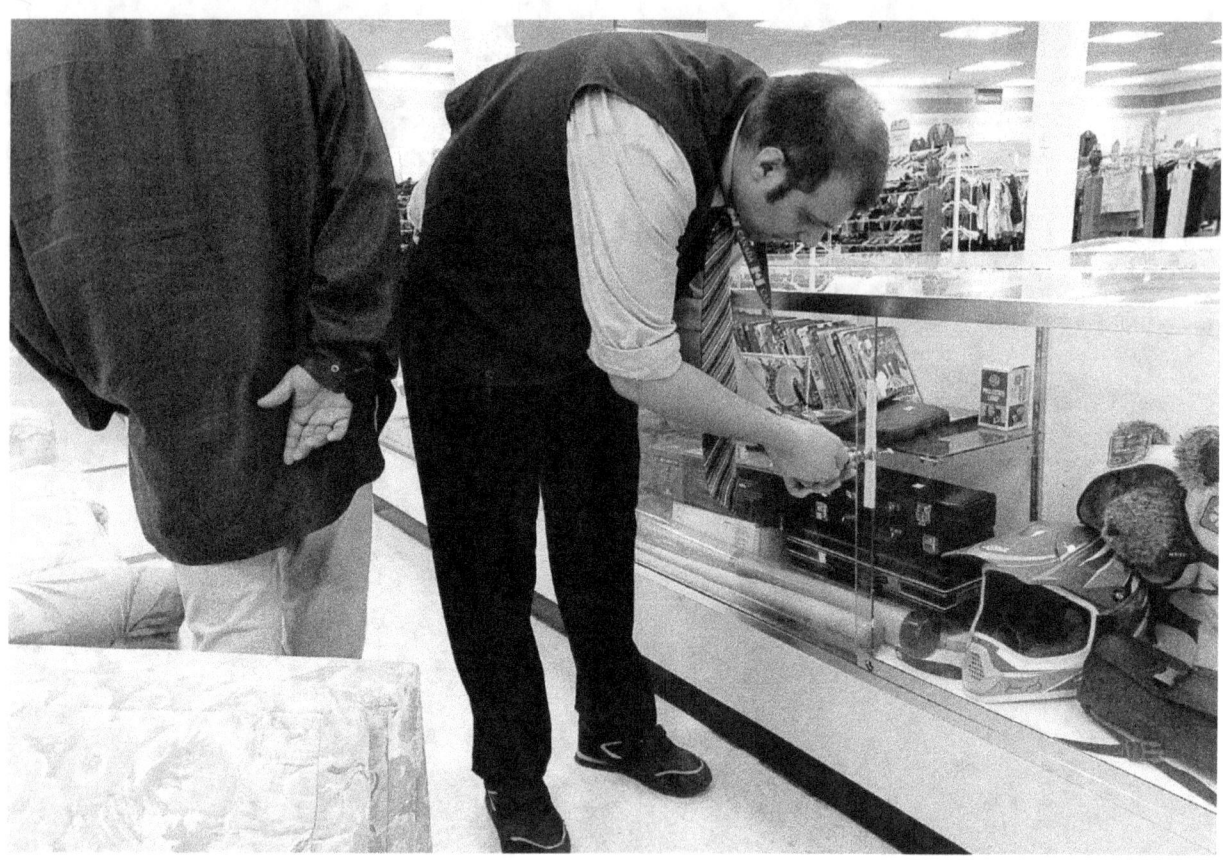

Mesa, Arizona

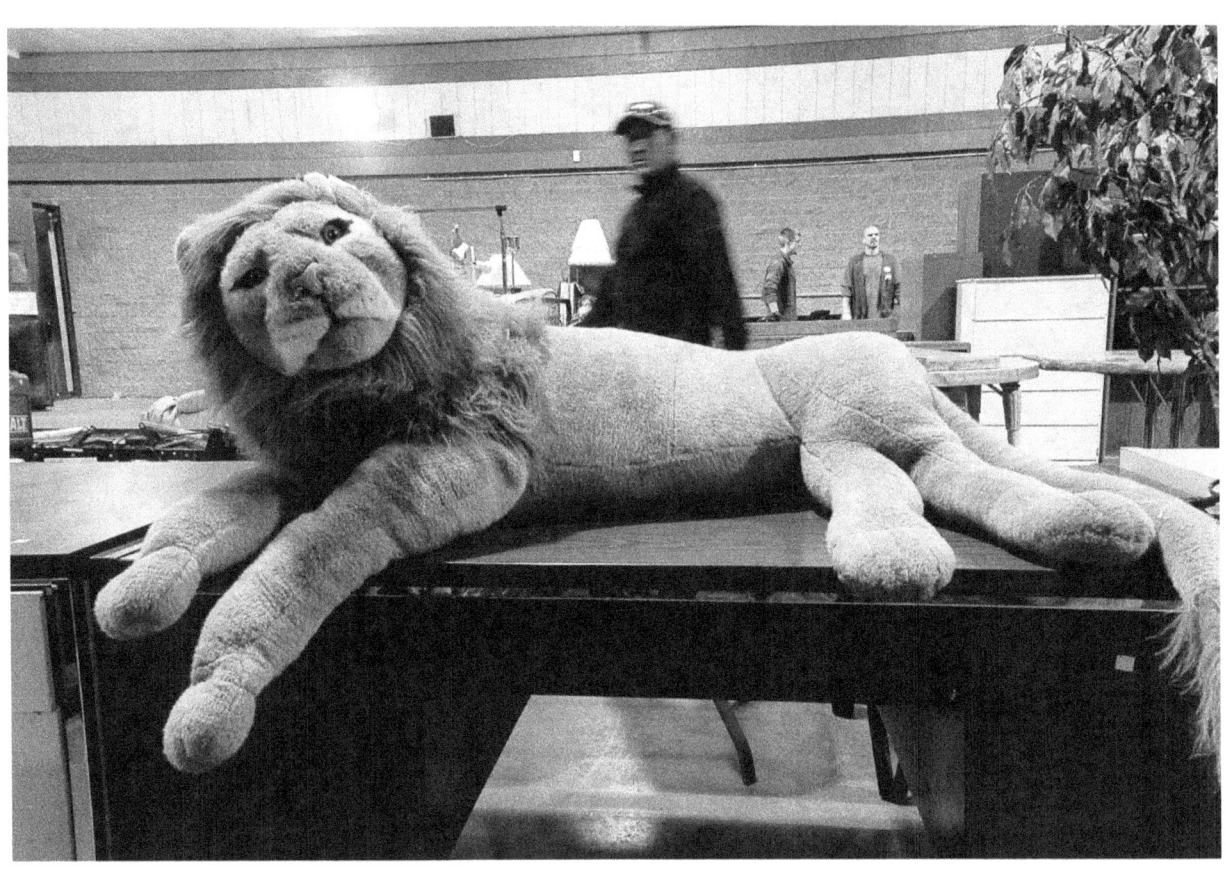

St. George, Utah

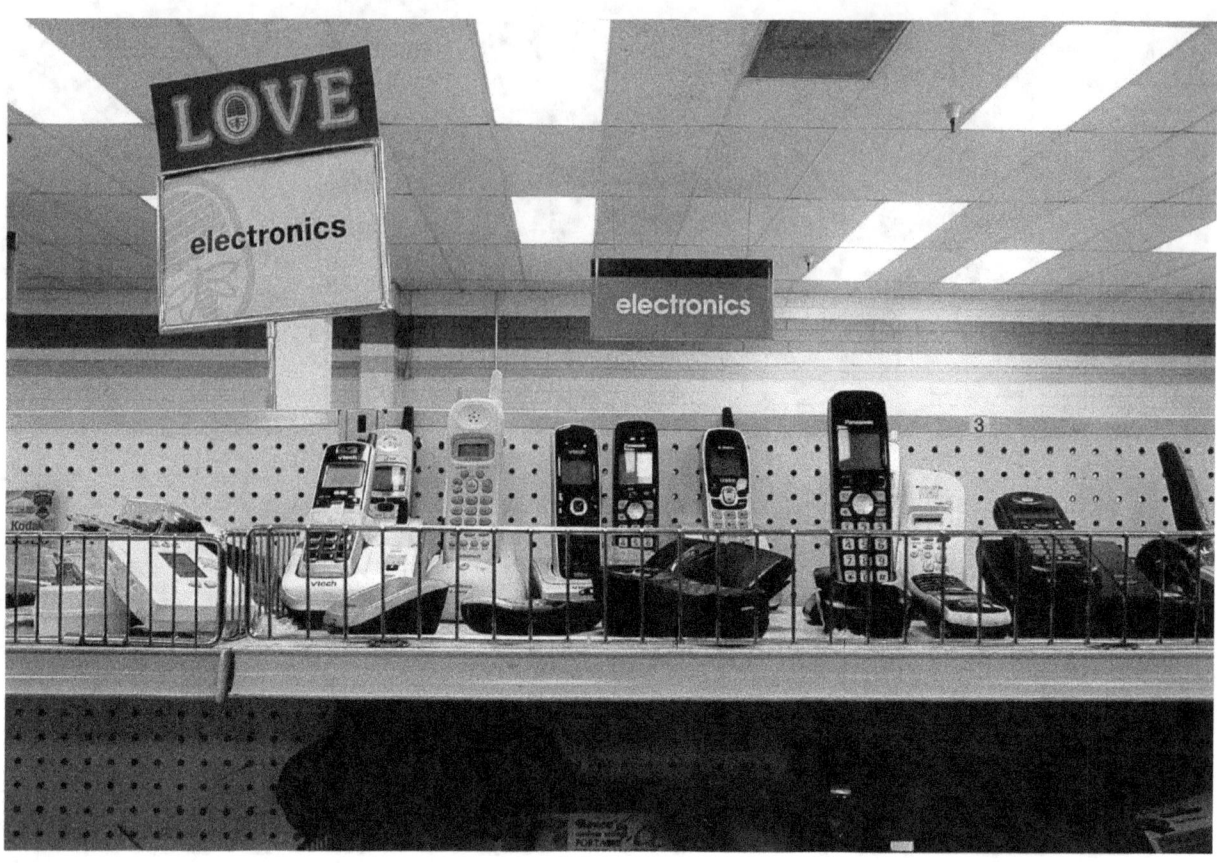

Mesa, Arizona

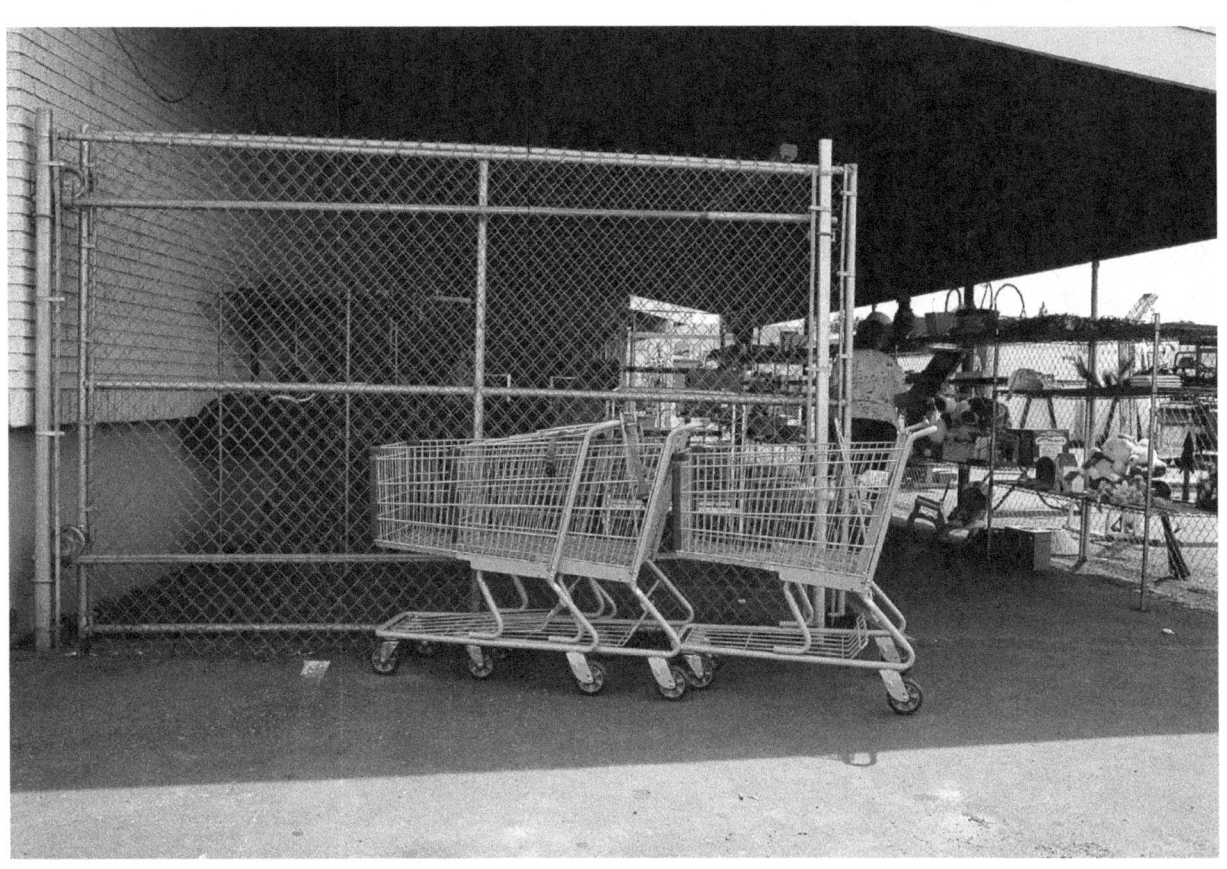

Richfield, Utah

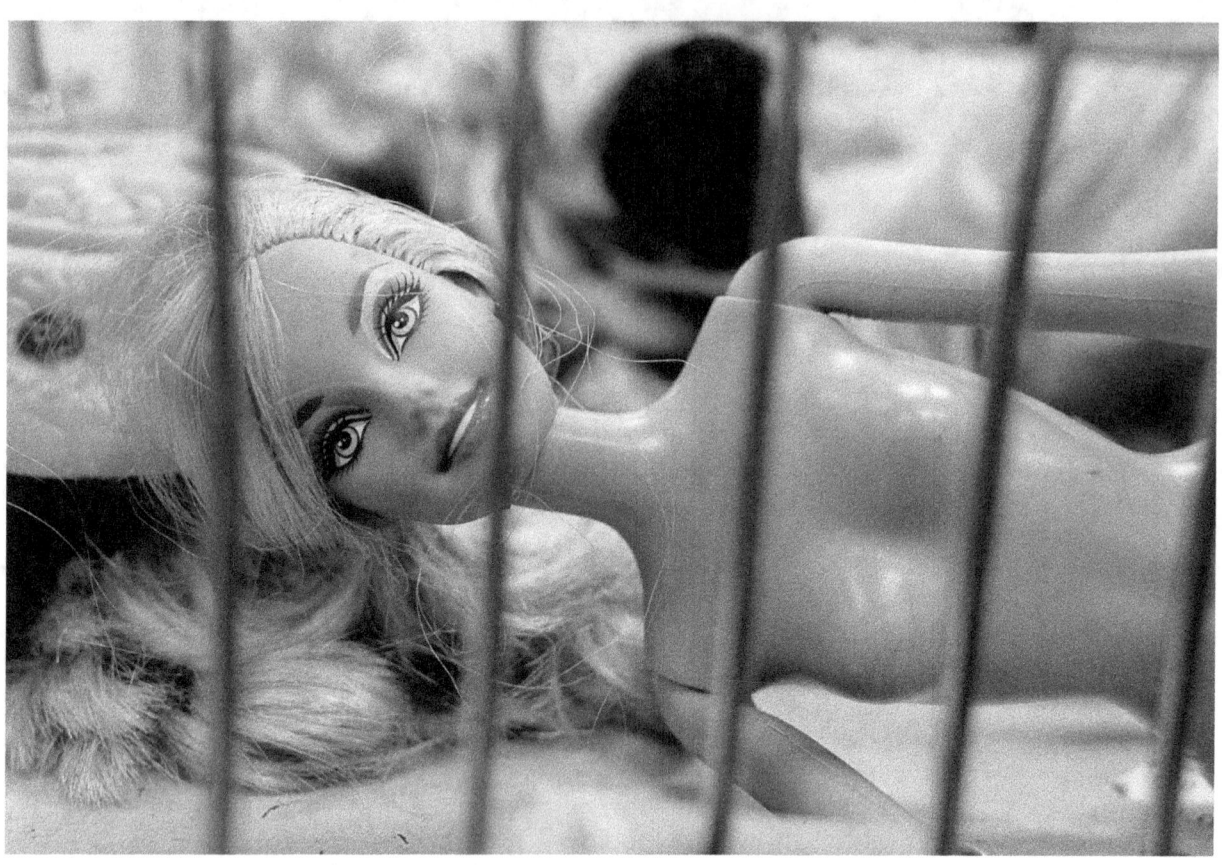

Provo, Utah

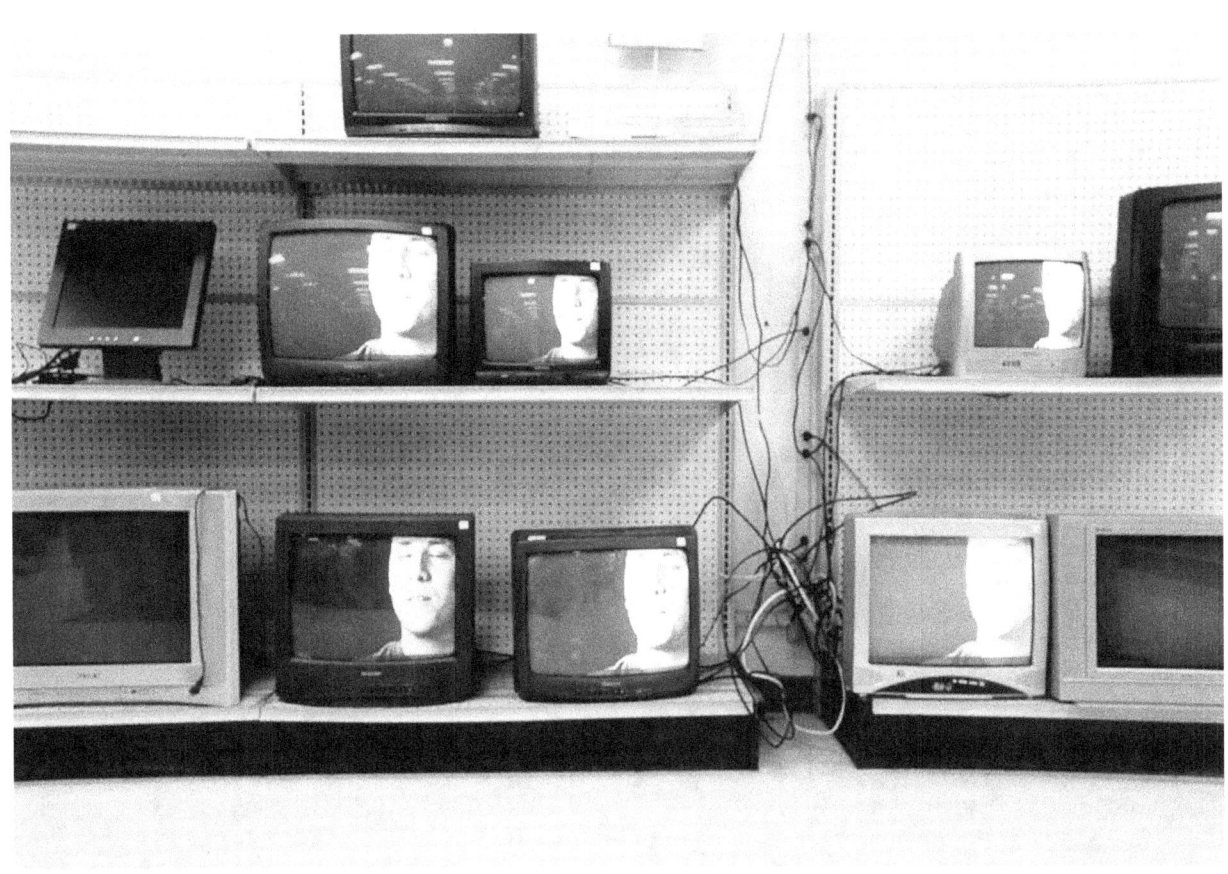

Blackfoot, Idaho

Opening Rush

If you ever get the chance to be at a Deseret Industries in the morning, a few minutes before they open, take it. It's an unforgettable freakshow.

My friend Bob works in IT and knows computers inside and out. Years ago, we used to go to the 10:00 am rush at the opening of the Provo, Utah, Deseret Industries. Bob knew most of the characters by name. There's people there looking for hard drives, old motherboards, and old video cards to sell on eBay. We liked to show up about fifteen minutes before opening.

Bob knew what some of the shoppers were looking for and which part of the store they were headed to. There were book nuts, stereo freaks, and vintage furniture junkies. There were 20 people waiting in front of the store for it to open. They greeted each other and talked about recent finds.

Time and again in almost every state, at almost every store, there's 20-30 people waiting for the doors to open so they can get a sweet deal on some esoteric piece of second hand junk only they know the value of. I thought it must only happen in Provo because it's one of the largest stores in the chain. I was wrong.

I've witnessed the opening rush at many stores. People race to the back. People argue before the doors open. People start banging on the doors right at 10:00. Banging on the doors of a thrift store. Begging to get in to a thrift store. It's a spectacle and I love it.

I always try to be at Deseret Industries a little before opening.

Shady Deals

At the Deseret Industries in Sacramento, California, I stepped into the men's room. While washing my hands, a late 20's heavy set Latino dude came in. He was wearing a black t-shirt, khaki shorts and sneakers. He was wearing a black daypack that seemed overloaded. It was bulging and sticking out off his back like it had too many books in it. He walked fast and went straight into a stall.

I heard the door lock and then I heard the toilet tank clank and rattle – that distinct sound of porcelain against porcelain. I briefly wondered what he was doing in there. He came out almost immediately.

I was drying my hands and as he exited the stall we made eye contact.

"Dude," he said to me, "someone made an awful mess in there," and he hustled out the door.

As we left the store just before closing we parked at the far corner of the parking lot to pause and make plans for the rest of the evening. While we were deciding and chatting a car pulled in and parked a few spots away. It was a black BMW. A new one. With gold wheels and tinted windows. It was there for a few minutes and white Mercedes Benz pulled in and parked right next to it. The Mercedes was new as well. With gold wheels and tinted windows. A young kid got out of the back doors of the BMW and went in to the Deseret Industries. He was gone less than five minutes. He came out, talked to the guy in the white Mercedes, got back in the BMW and both cars left.

The whole episode was odd. Then I remembered the character in the bathroom with the backpack and the toilet tank lid rattling. As the cars left the parking lot, I realized I may have witnessed a slick drug deal in the parking lot of a Mormon-owned second hand store.

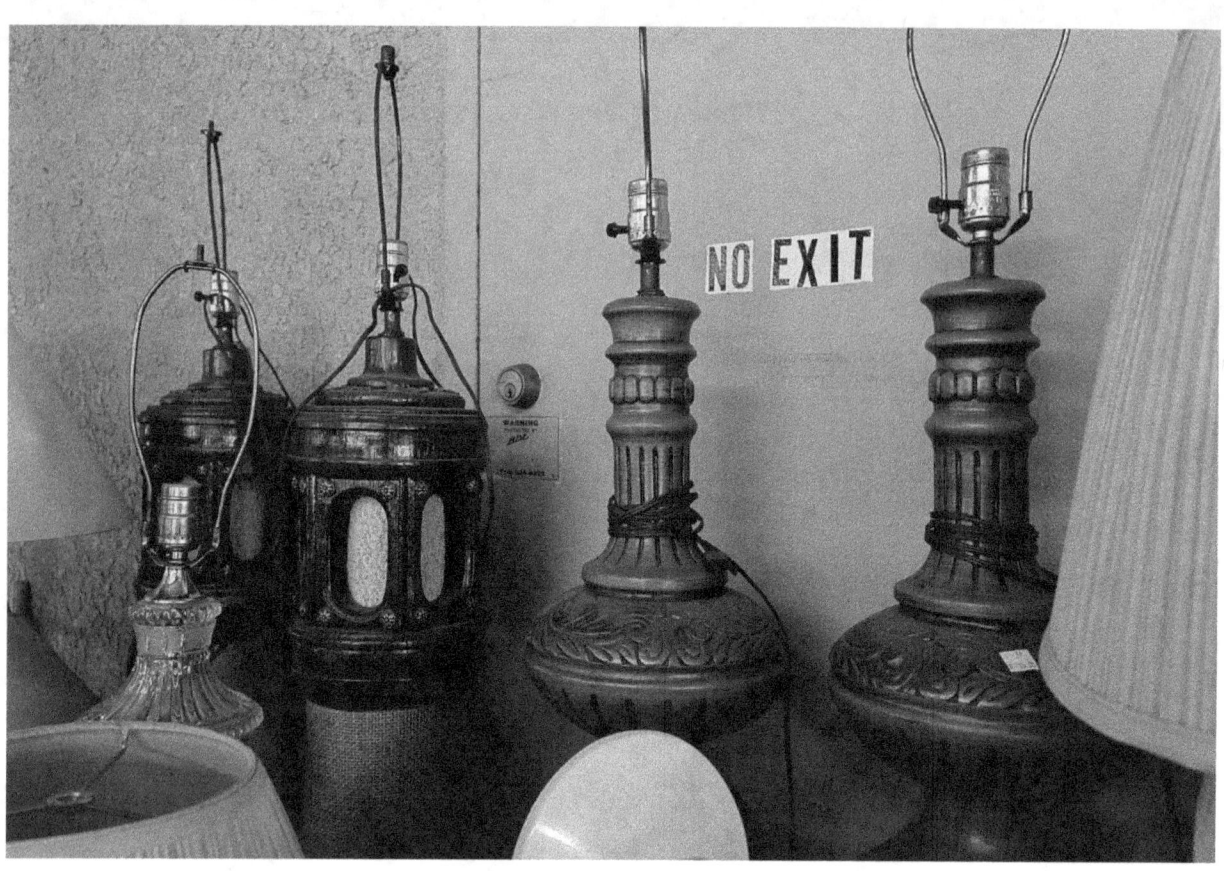

Calimesa, California

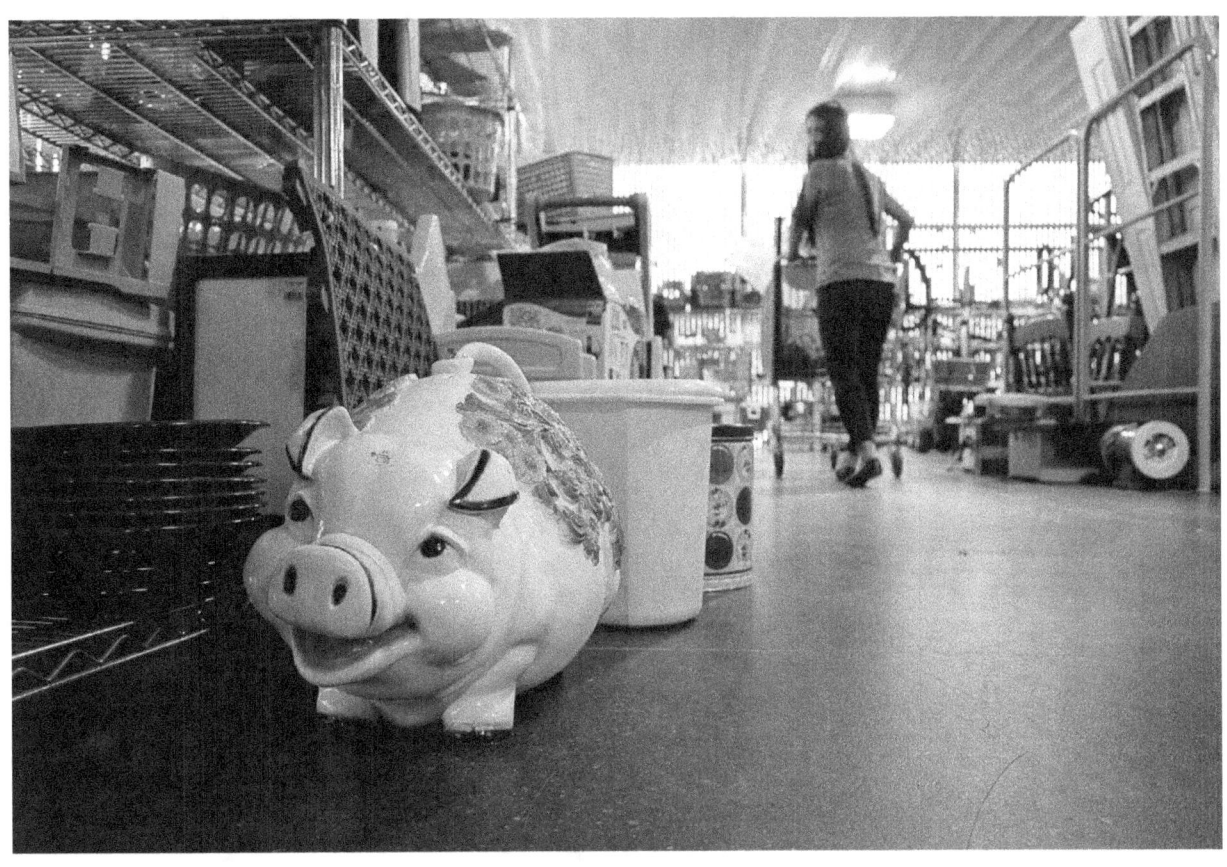

Sandy, Utah

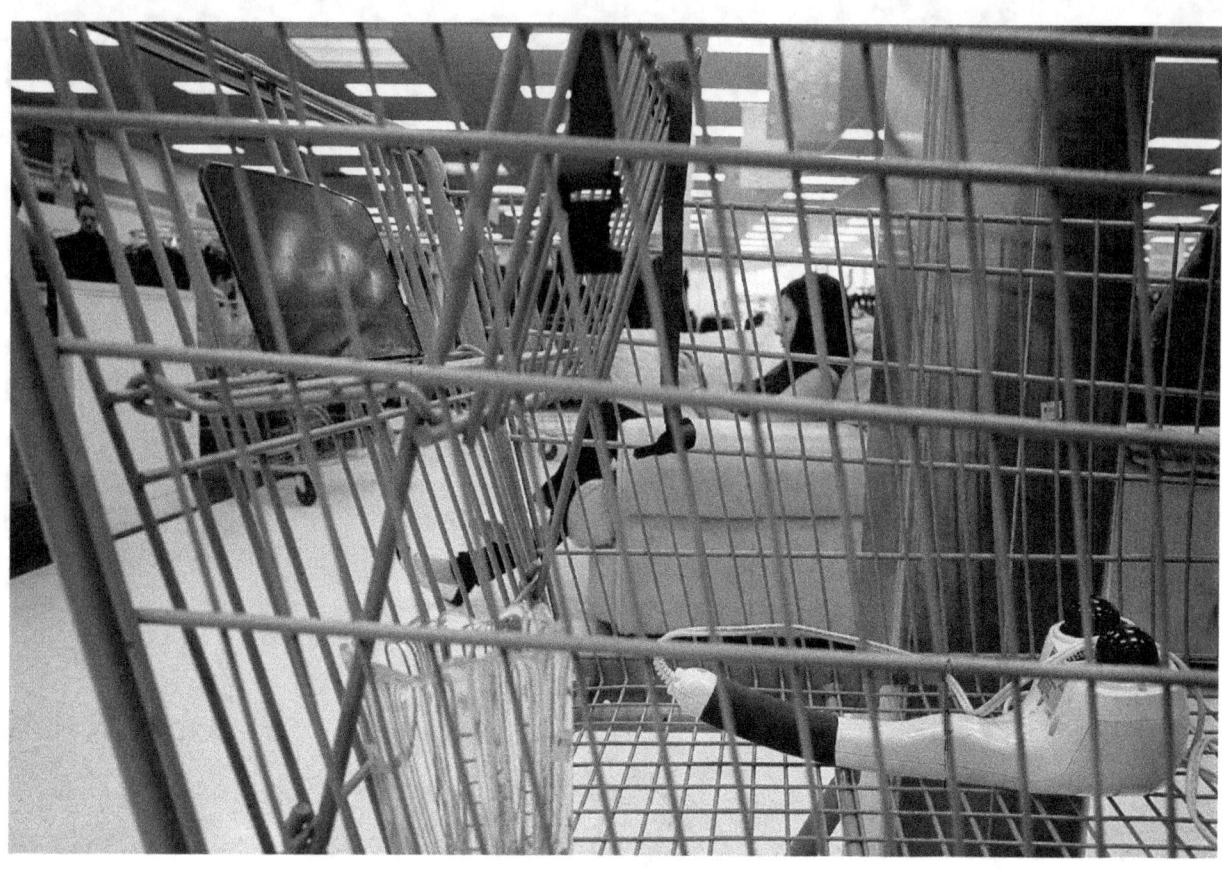

Sugarhouse, Utah

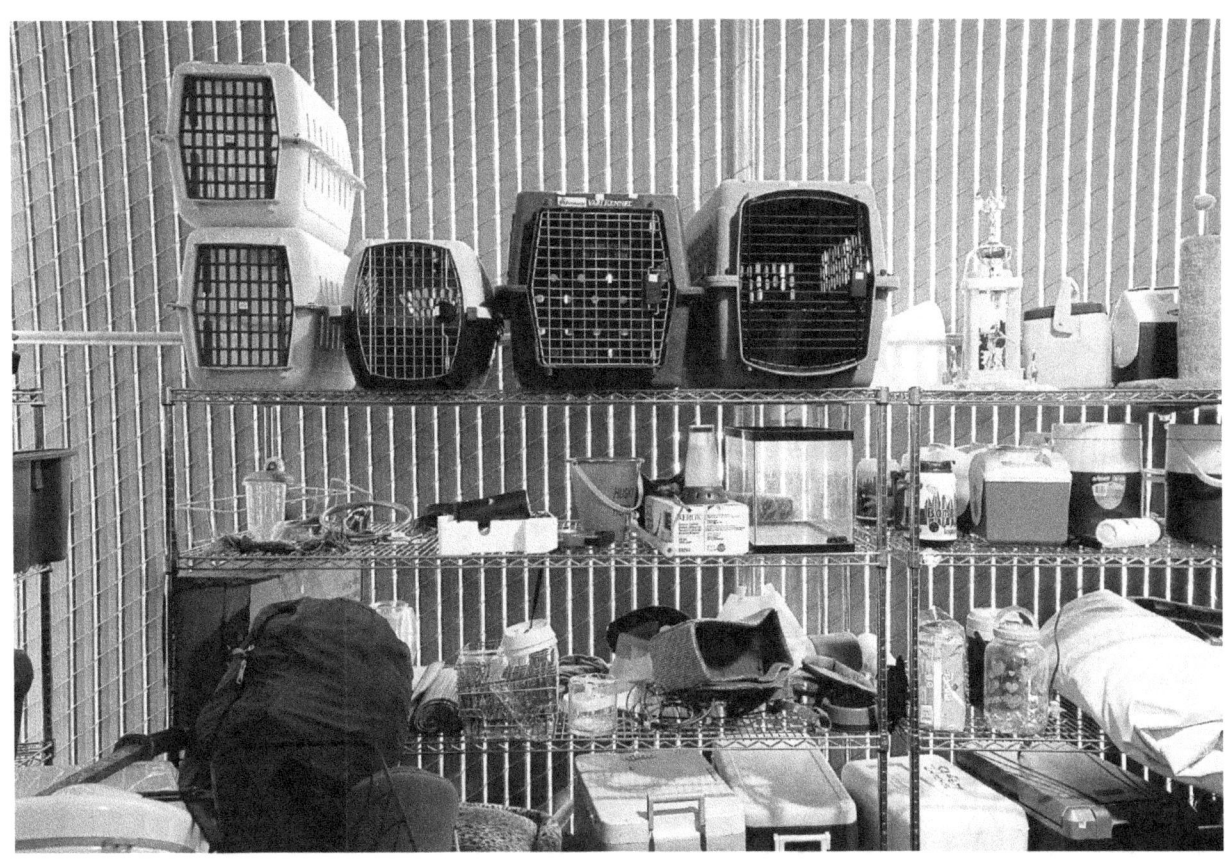

Sandy, Utah

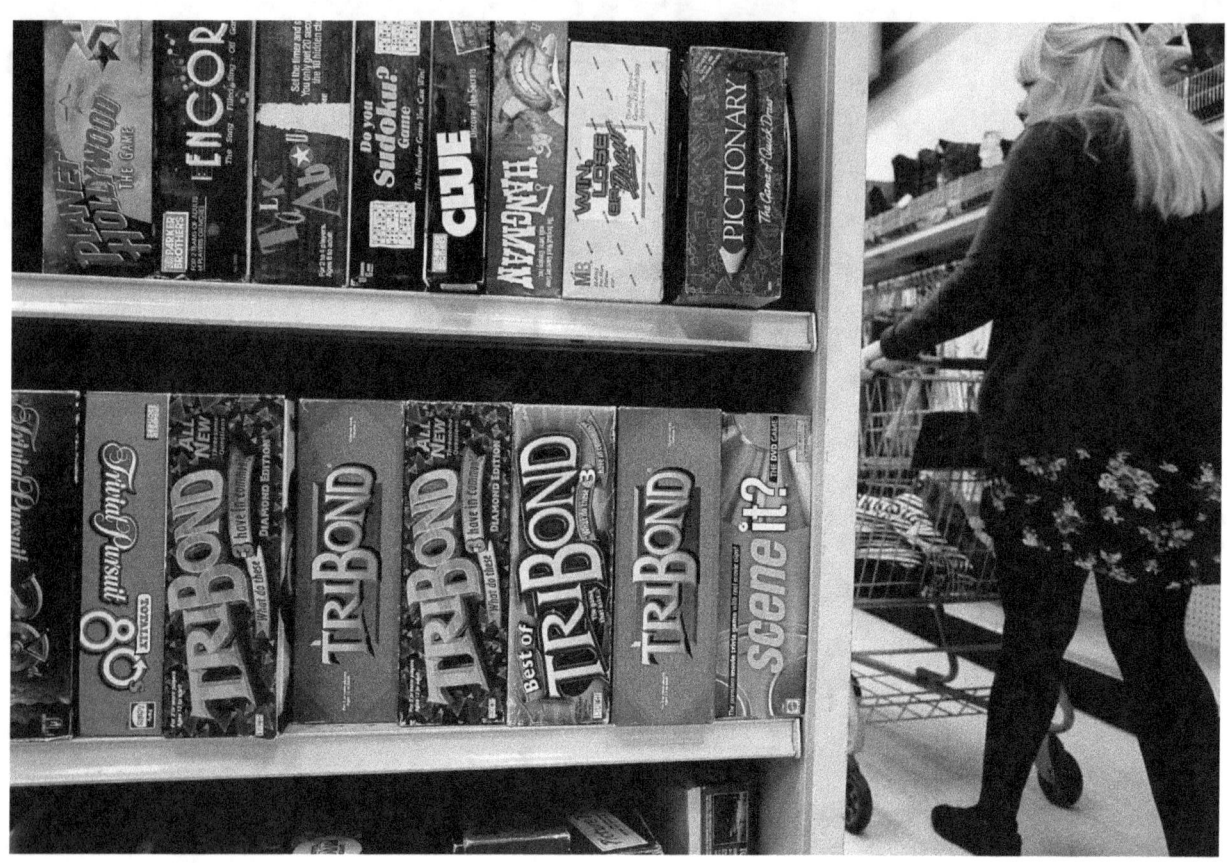

Sugarhouse, Utah

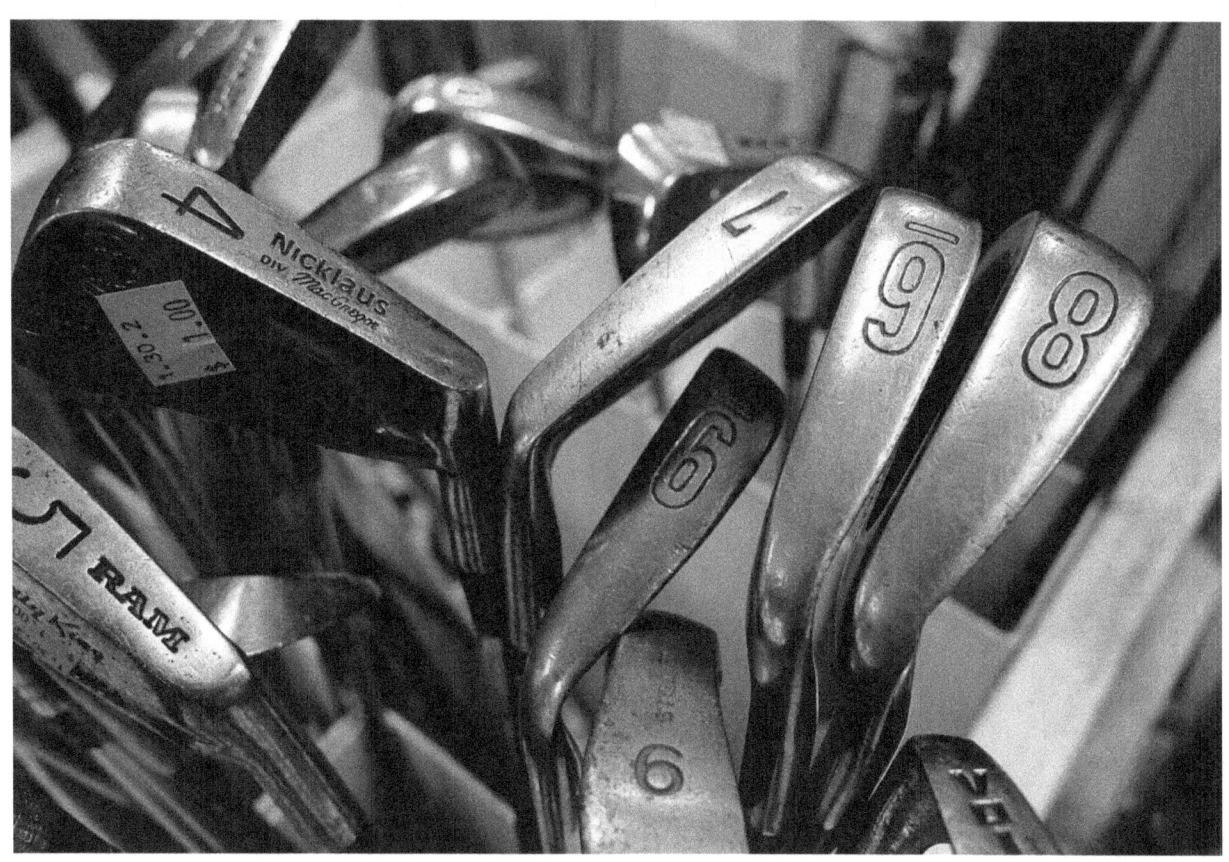

Federal Way, Washington

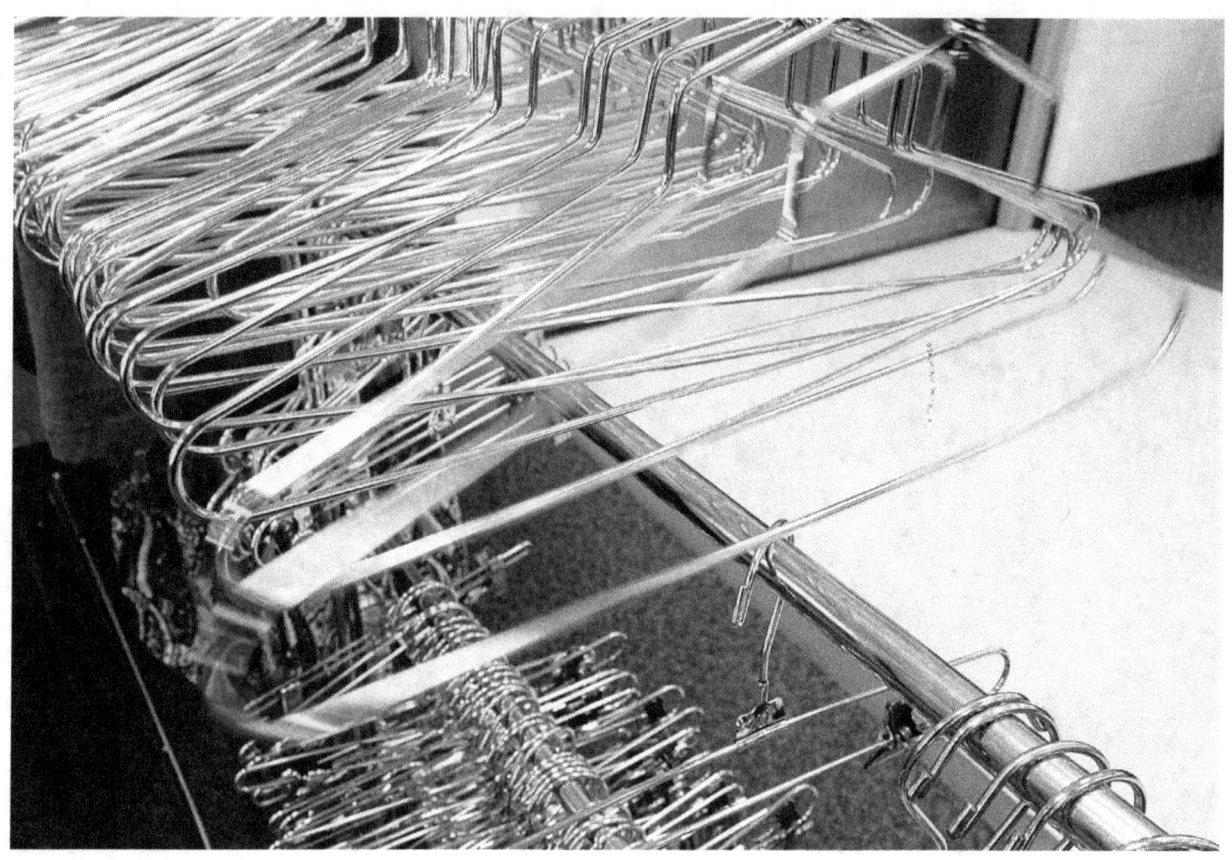

Los Angeles, California

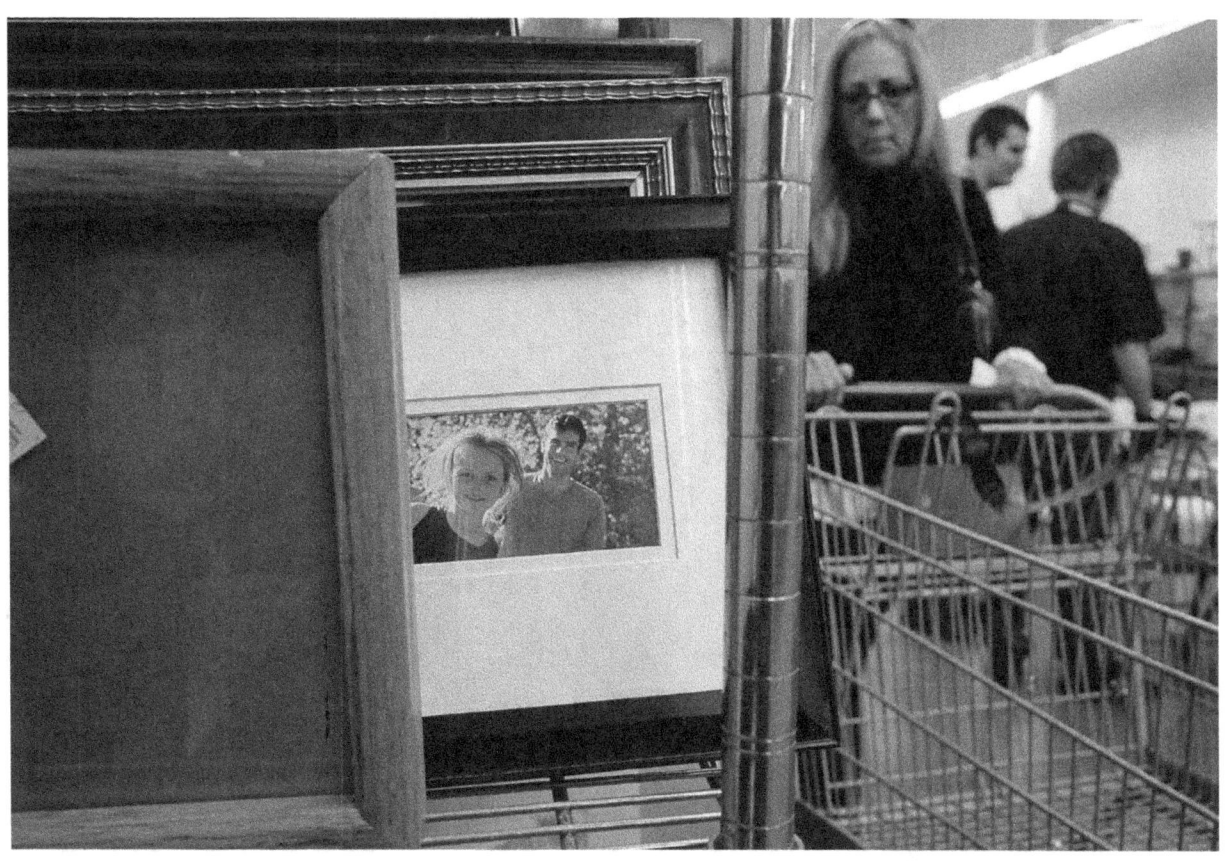

Sugarhouse, Utah

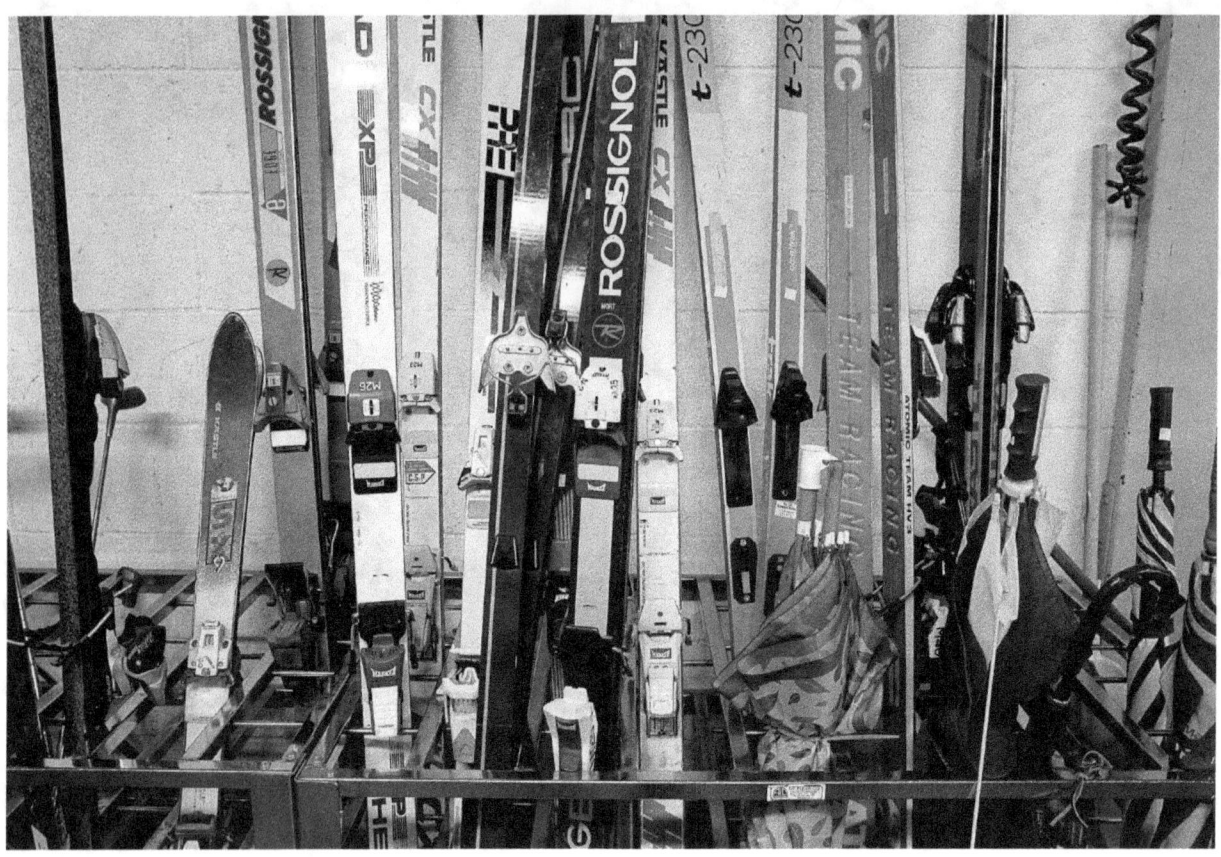

Provo, Utah

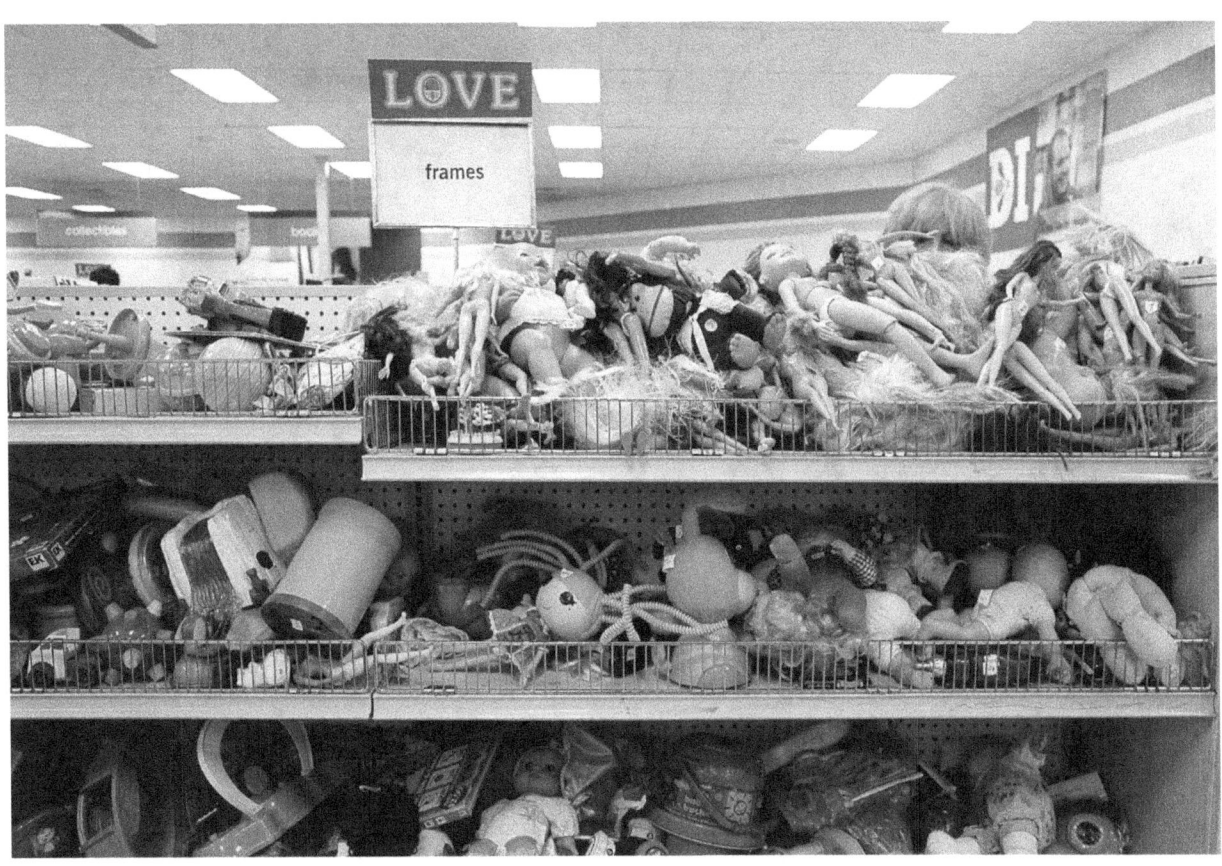

Welfare Square, Utah

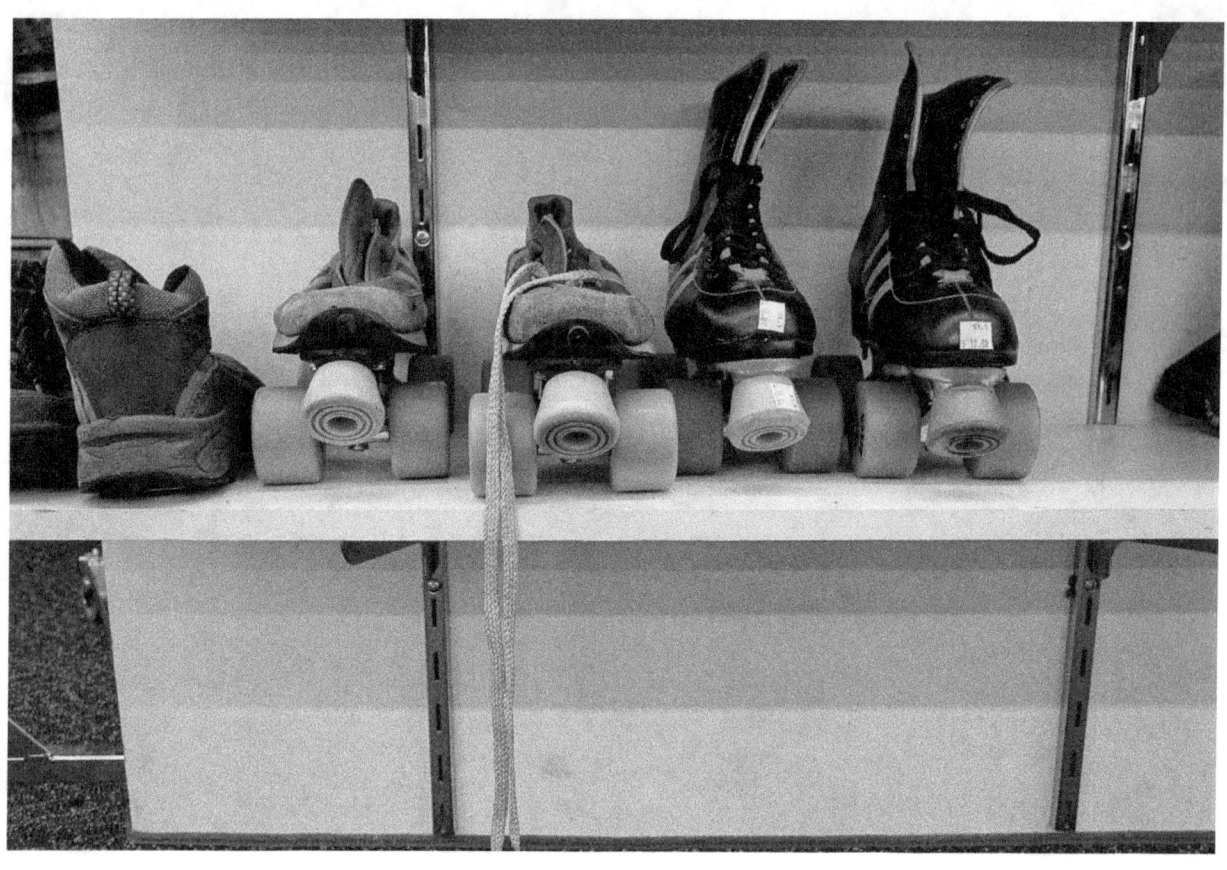

Brigham City, Utah

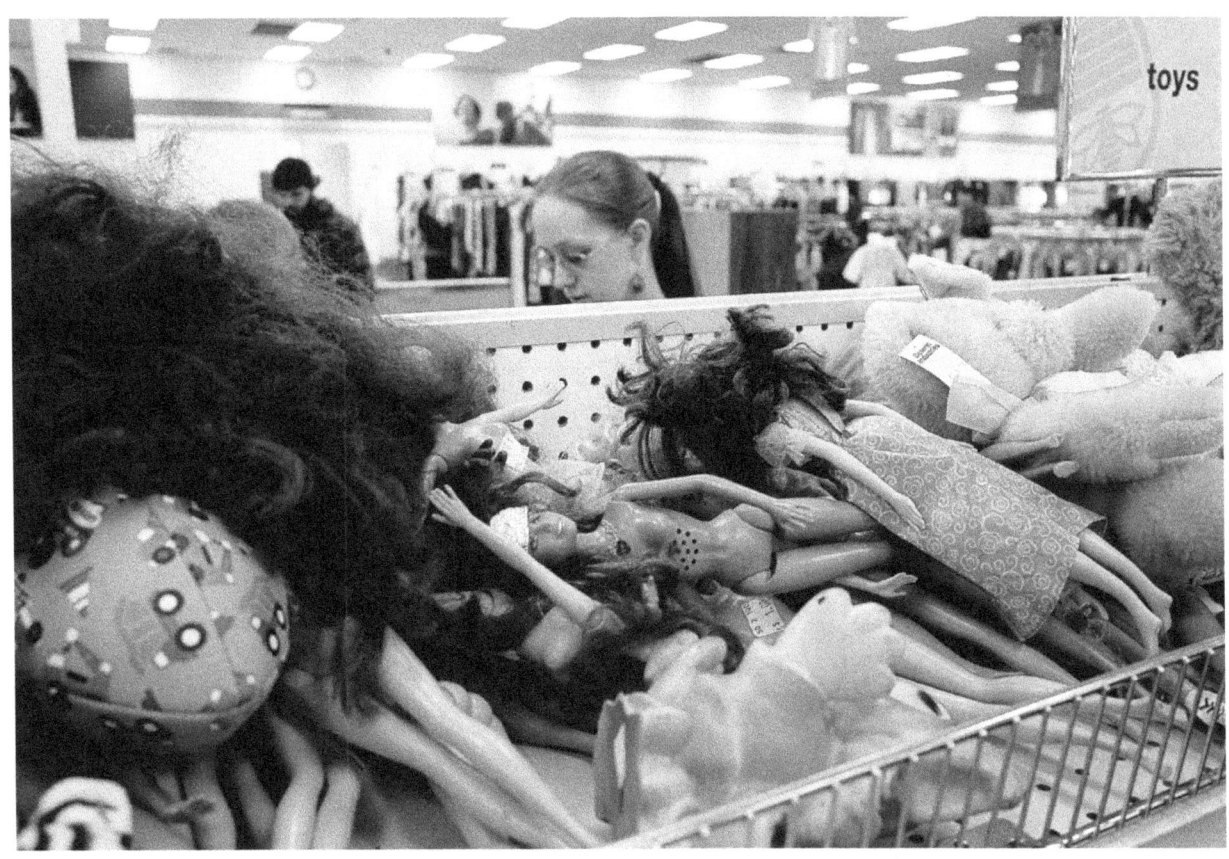

Logan, Utah

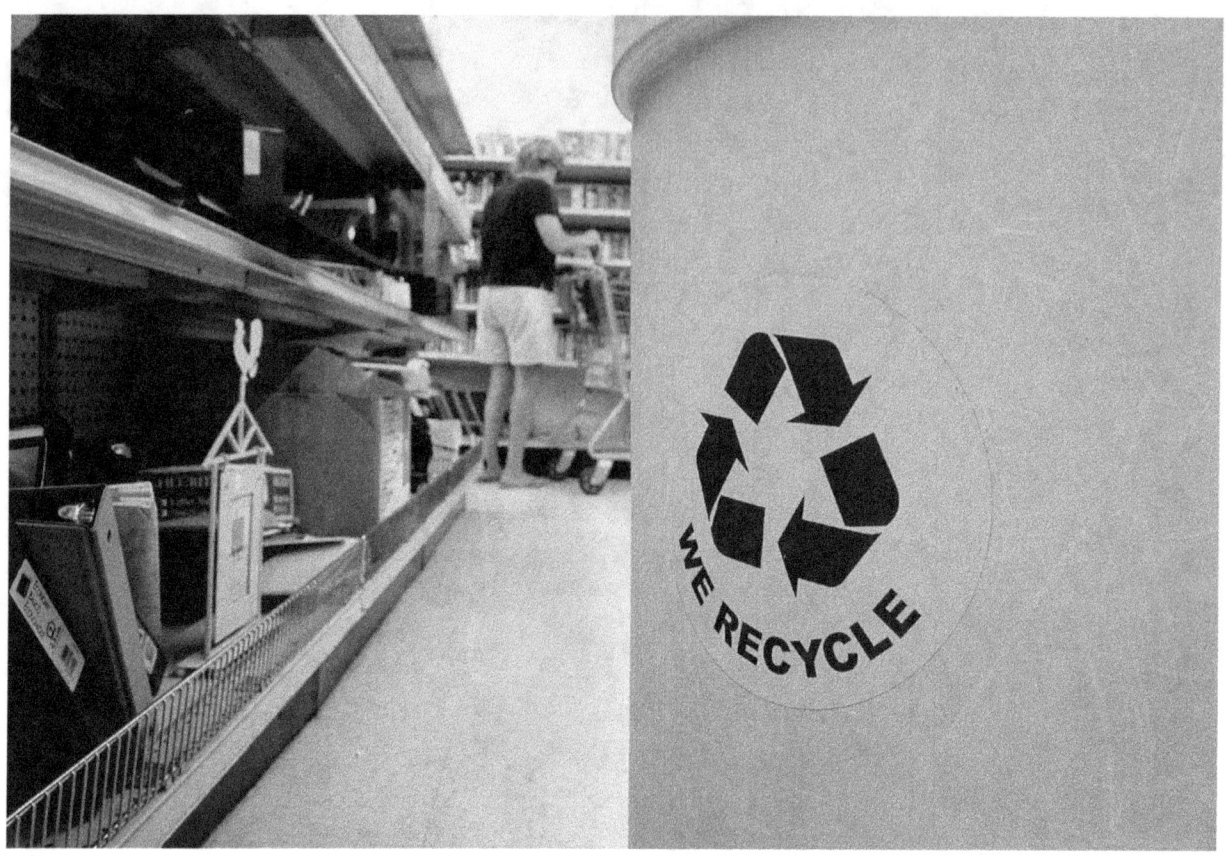

Nampa, Idaho

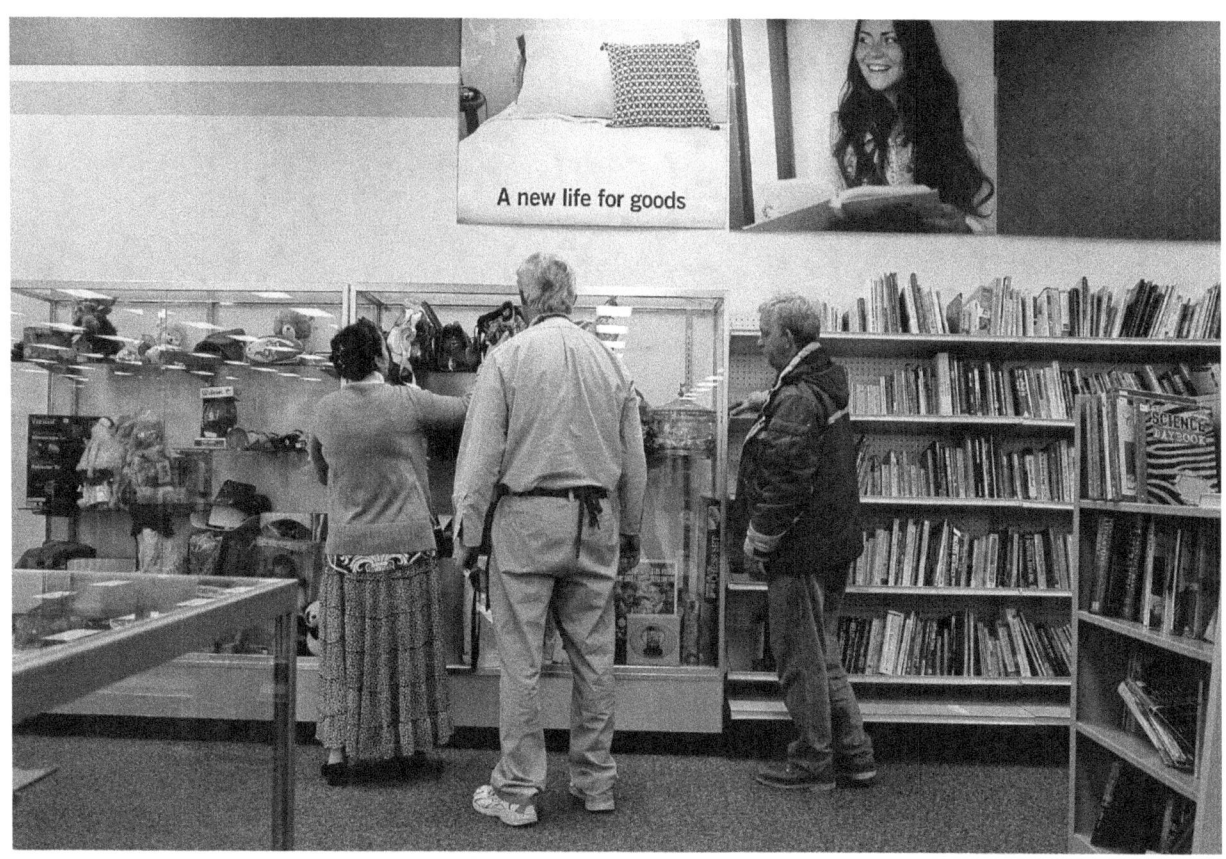

Welfare Square, Utah

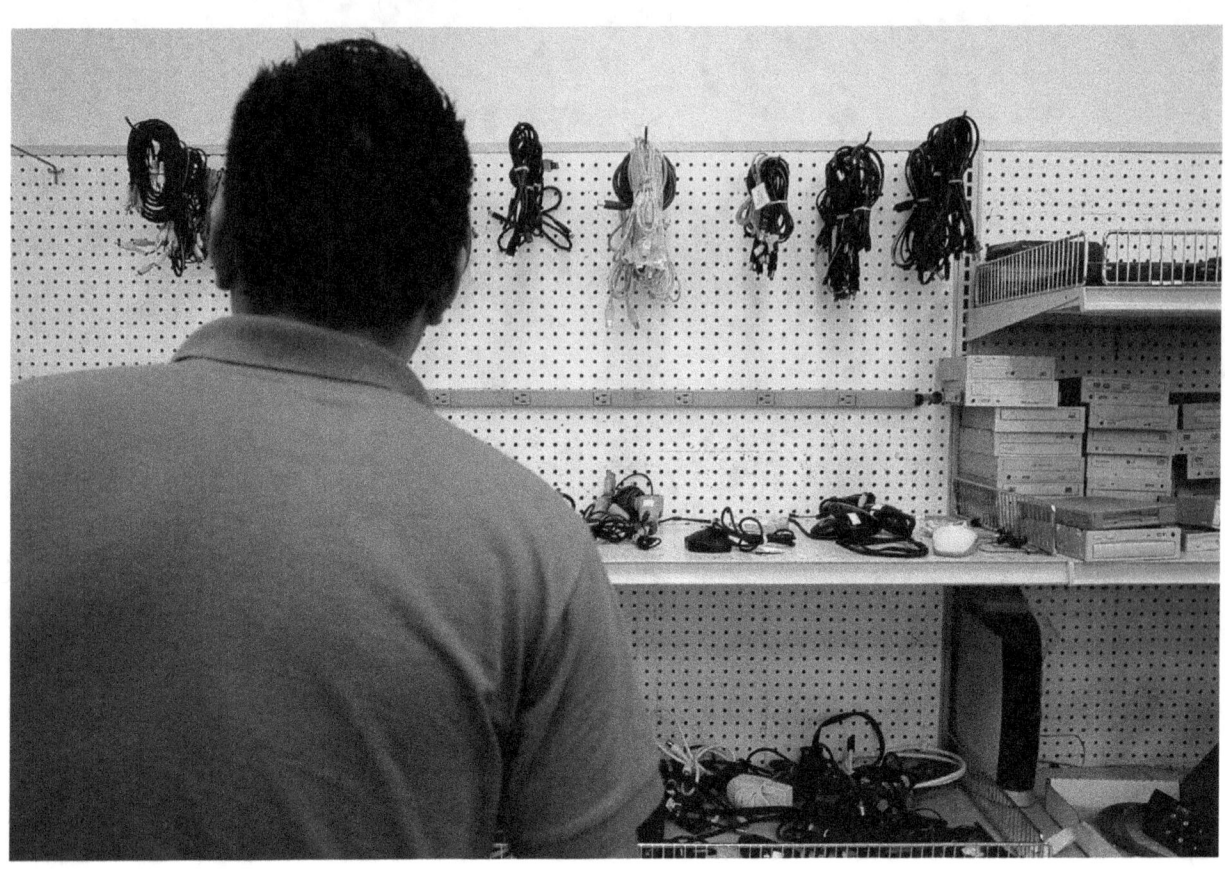

Murray, Utah

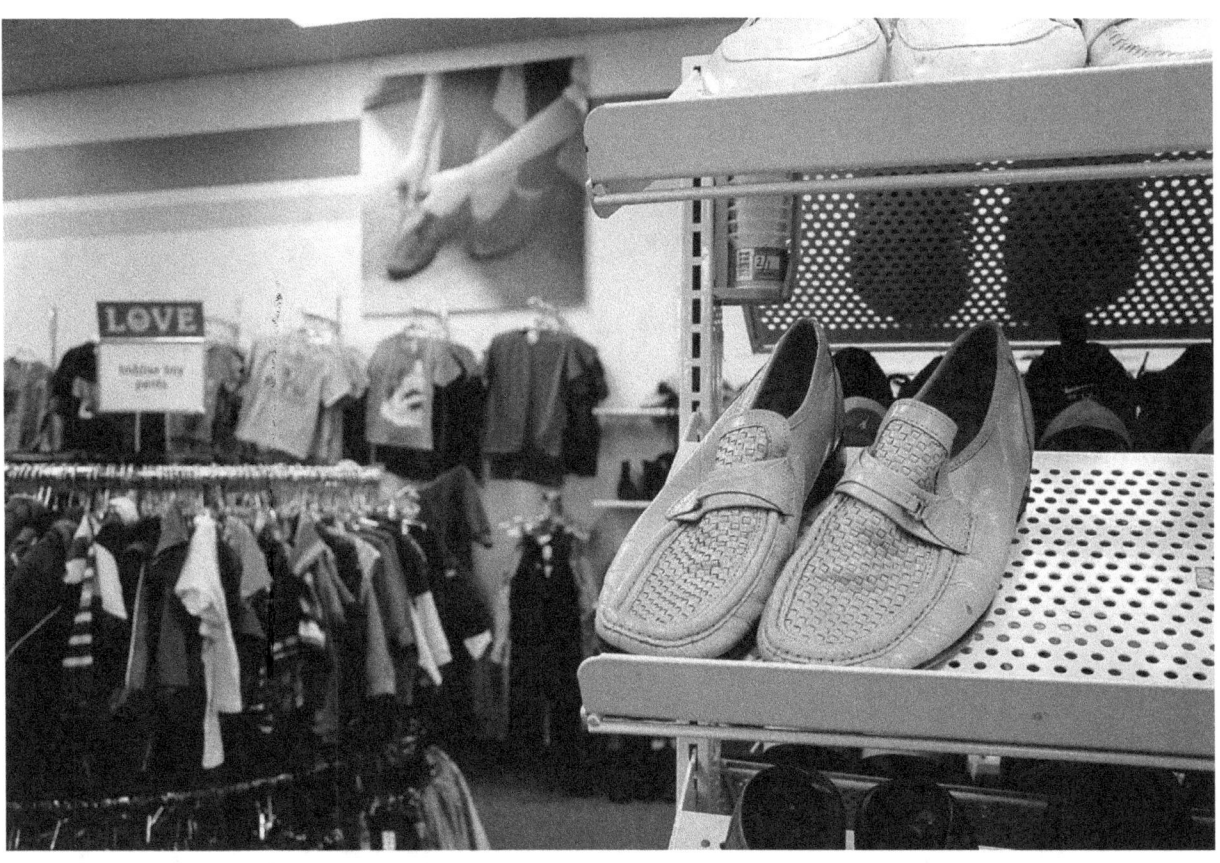

Welfare Square, Utah

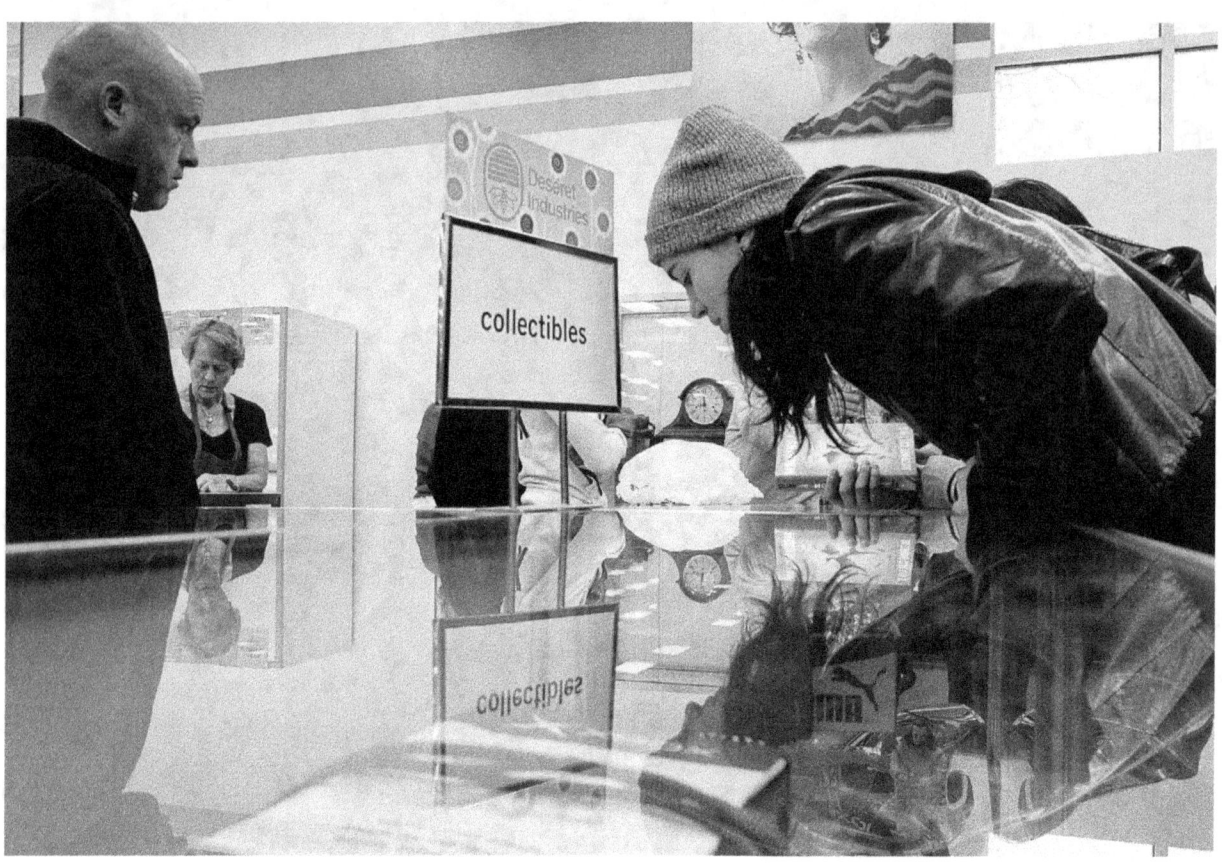

Sugarhouse, Utah

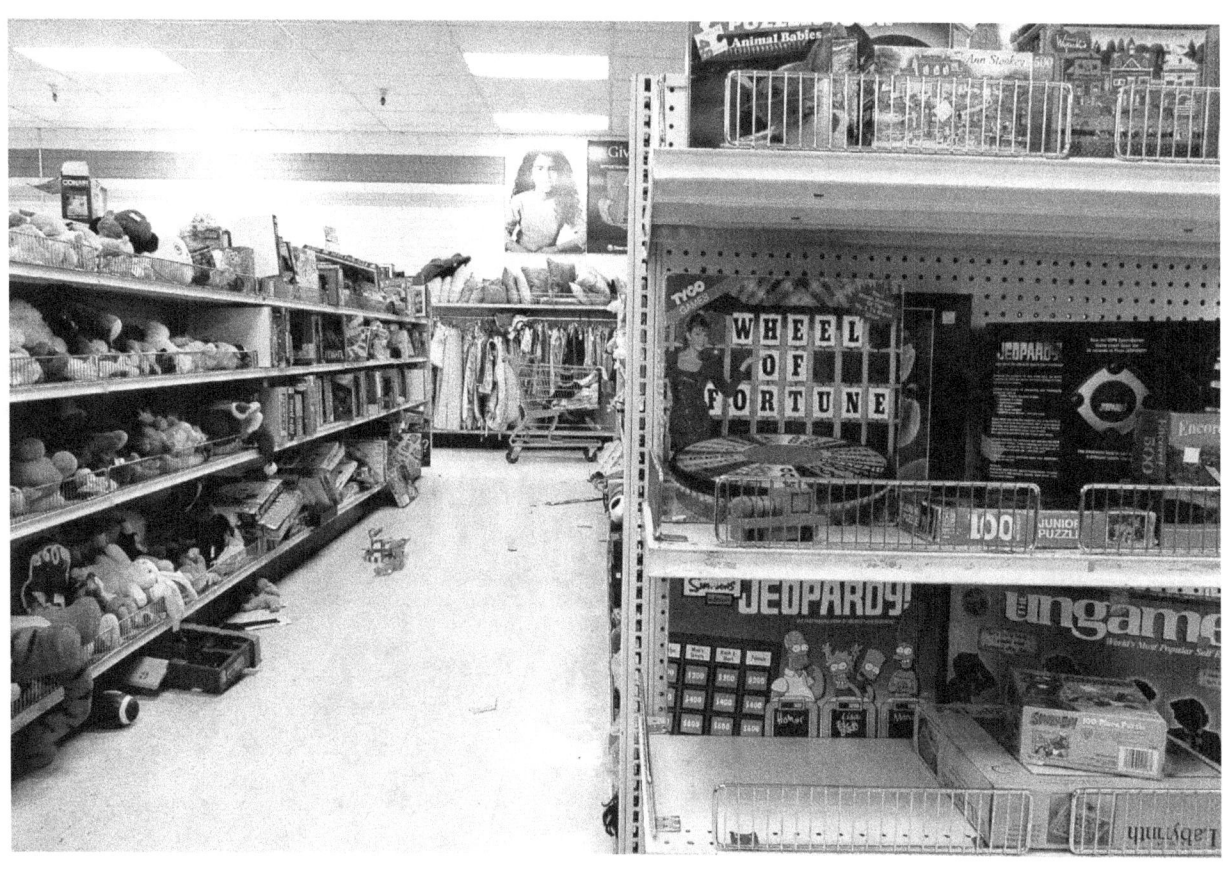

Mesa, Arizona

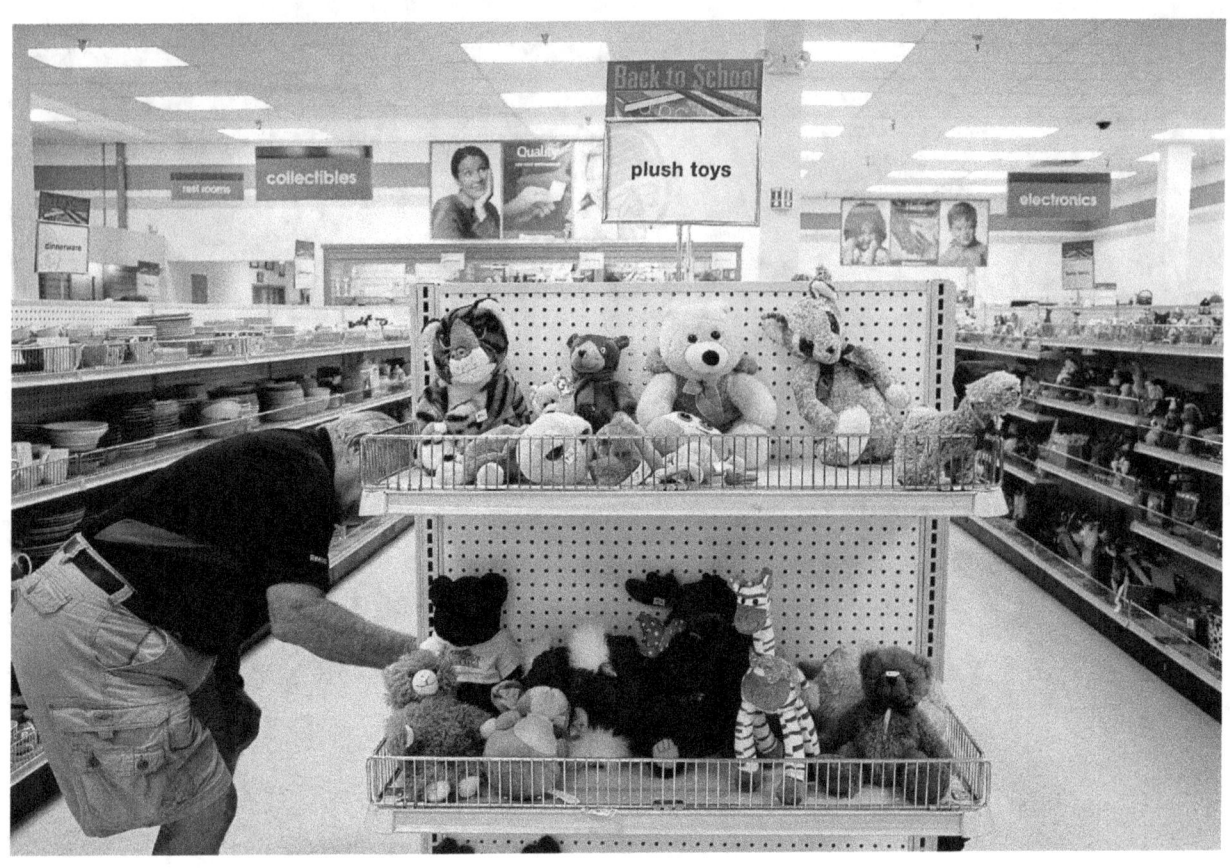

Seattle, Washington

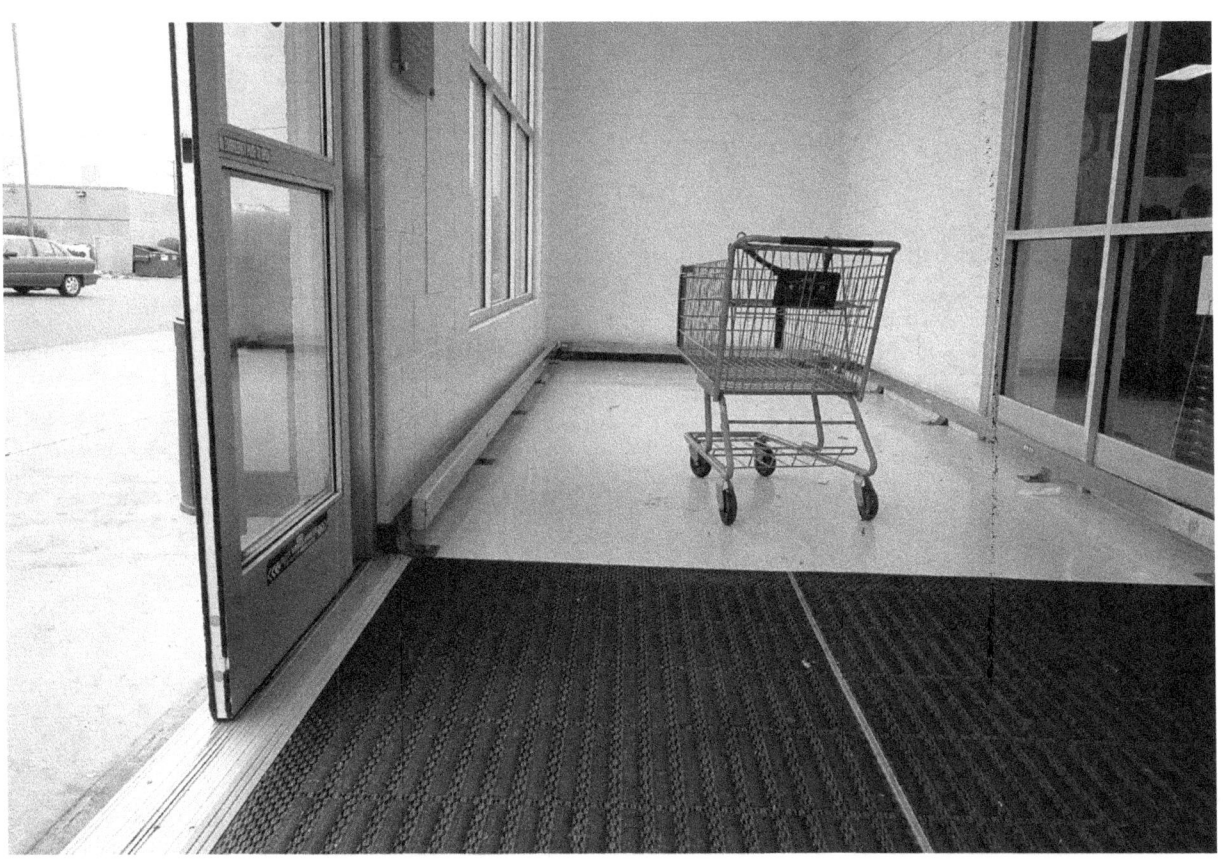

Sugarhouse, Utah

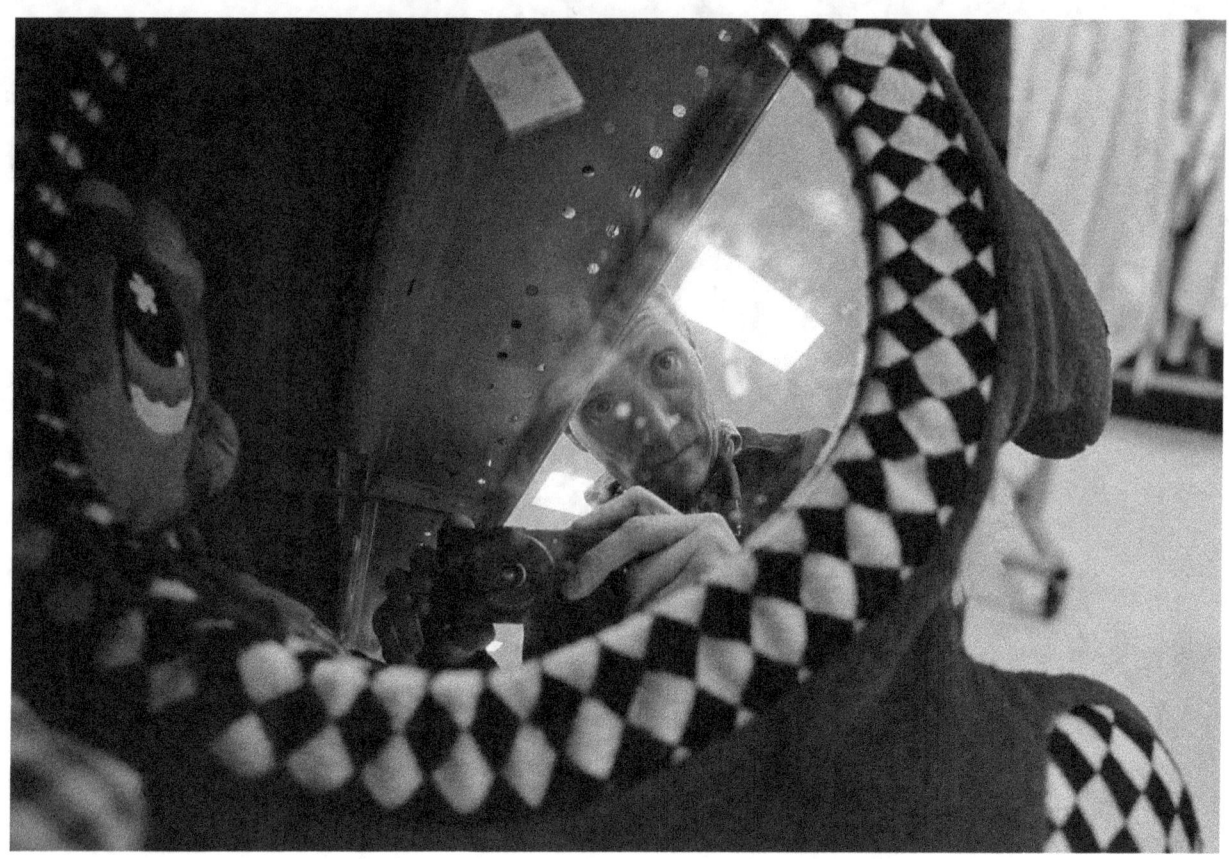

Murray, Utah

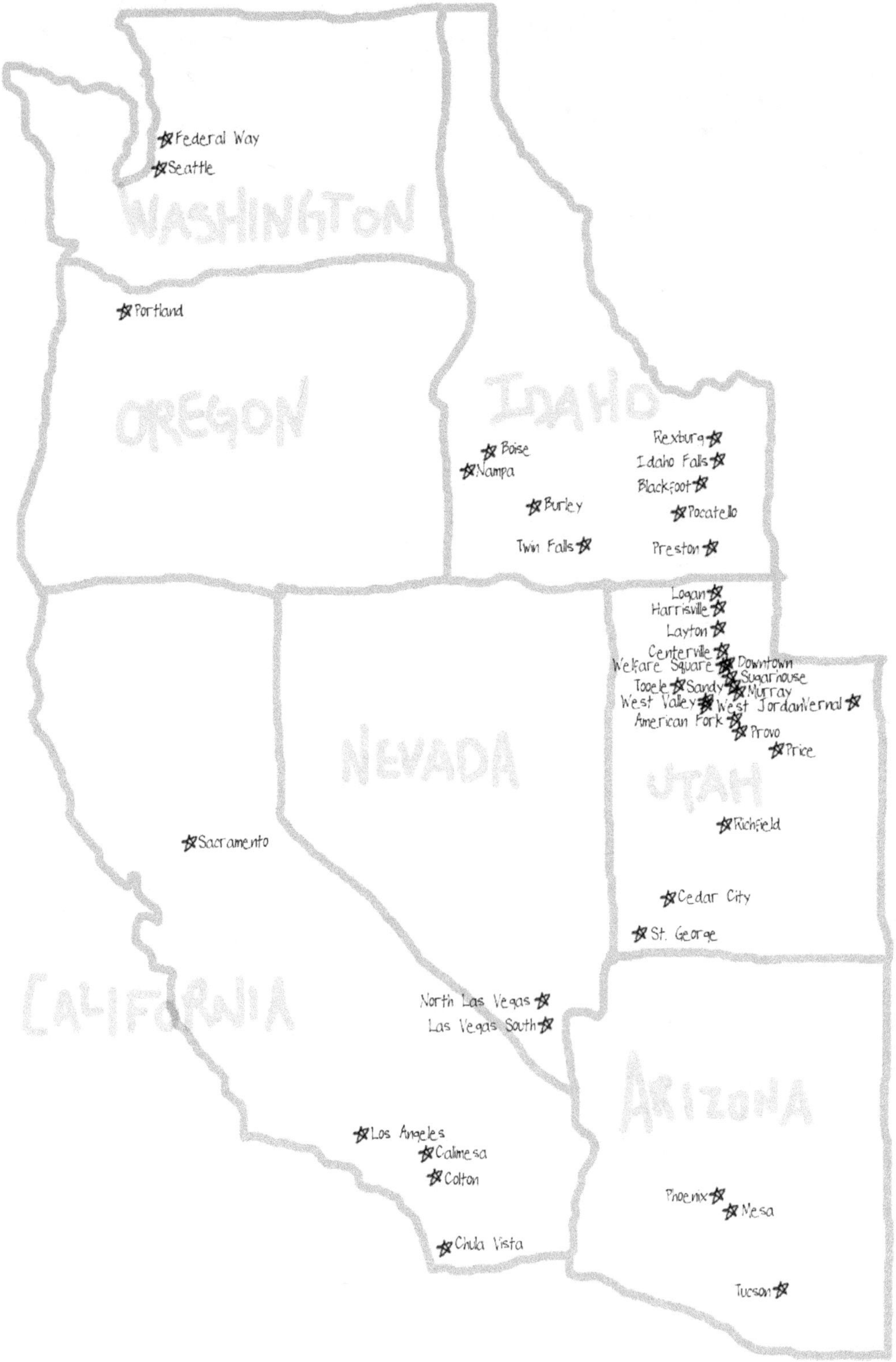

Federal Way
Seattle
WASHINGTON

Portland

OREGON

IDAHO

Boise
Nampa
Burley
Twin Falls

Rexburg
Idaho Falls
Blackfoot
Pocatello
Preston

Logan
Harrisville
Layton
Centerville
Welfare Square
Tooele
Sandy
West Valley
American Fork
Provo
Price

Downtown
Sugarhouse
Murray
West Jordan Vernal

NEVADA

Sacramento

UTAH

Richfield

Cedar City

St. George

CALIFORNIA

North Las Vegas
Las Vegas South

ARIZONA

Los Angeles
Calimesa
Colton

Chula Vista

Phoenix
Mesa

Tucson

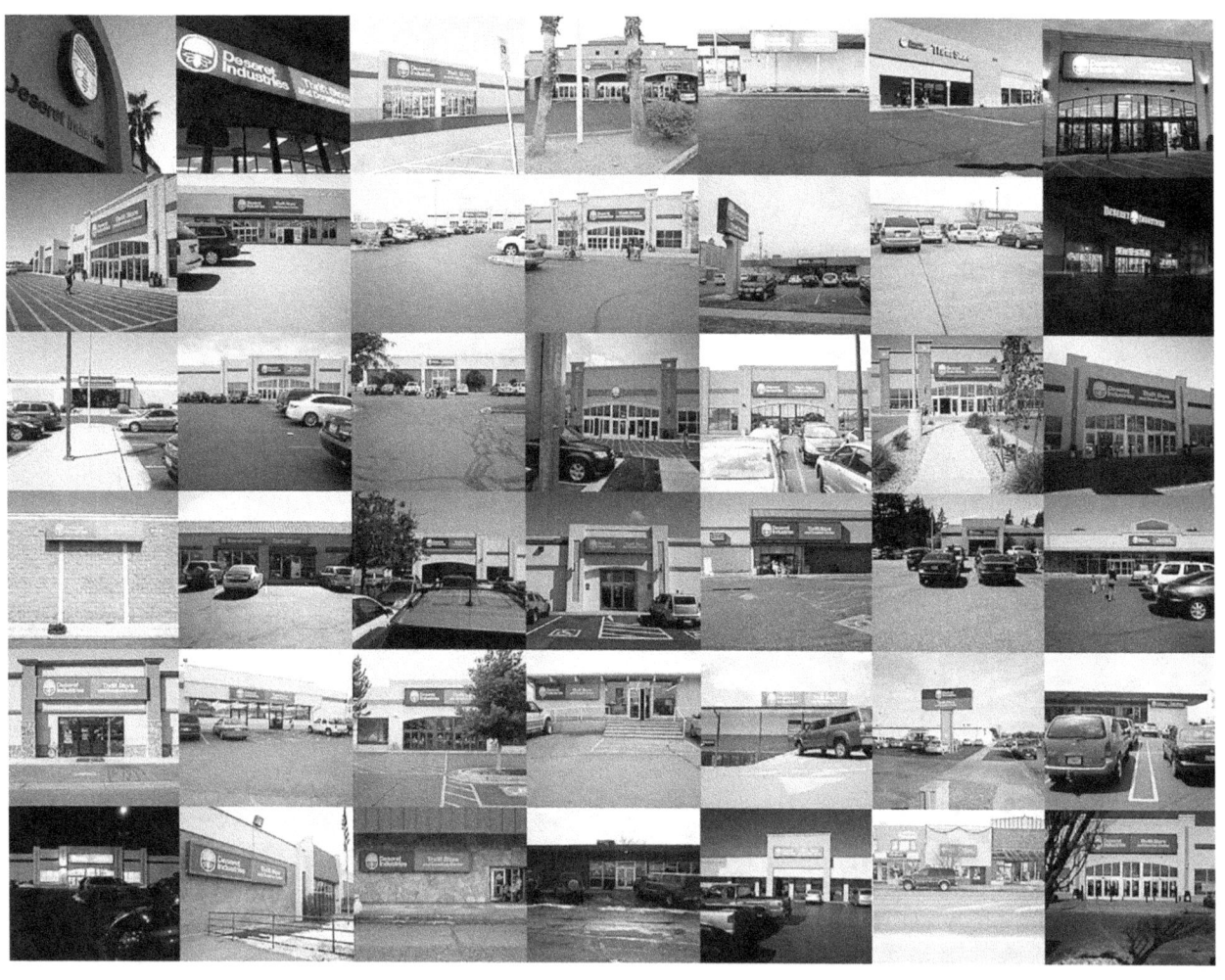

Deseret Industries 42 Storefronts

Thanks for looking.

There's a feeling that accompanies thrift shopping. A smell too. A weird, funky smell. Like a couch that's been buried in old gym socks and elderly women's floral print jackets and recently uncovered. It's a moth ball smell. An old perfume and stagnant dust smell. There's a hint of locker room.

At times the smell is overpowering and objectionable. Other times it's a mild background smell. It takes a lot of hand sanitizer to get rid of it.

Buying clothes in a thrift store takes patience and guts. Patience because the gems are there, but they're few and far between. Guts because you really have to spend some time in there and try stuff on. I read somewhere the cardinal rule of thrift shopping; don't buy it unless you absolutely love it. I can't say I bought something at every store, but I ended this journey with more flannel shirts than I had when I started.

I drove 7500+ miles - many with a pregnant wife and two small kids, and later with two small kids and an infant. I shot over 3500 photos. If you've been to a Deseret Industries, I hope you'll find the photos familiar. If you haven't, it's okay, most thrift stores are similar in that they serve as the last stop for our junk before it goes to the dump. It's a plea for relevance, a plea for one last chance. It's an way to throw things away while feeling a little bit less guilty.

My hope is you enjoyed the photos. I wish I could impart the smell and feel of old clothes, but photos will have to suffice.